The Heart of a Morning Paper beats online

How to organize the content workflow in a modern media company

Pit Gottschalk

Two Stones Publishing, Berlin
1. Auflage 2010

ISBN 978-1-4466-8738-3

Table of Contents

1. Introduction

On January 27th, 2010, Steve Jobs, chairman and CEO of Apple Inc., publicly announced the up-coming launch of the iPad, a multi-media device well designed for publishing newspaper content digitally.[1] Instantly, newspaper companies from all over the world praised the iPad as the one and only solution to rescue their print business, and claimed that soon they would be in the position to distribute content in this new digital way.[2] This is exactly the topic of this research: Are the newspaper companies really prepared for the new digital age?

86 percent of 704 senior editors from all over the world believe integrated print and online newsrooms will become the norm, and 83 percent believe journalists will be expected to be able to produce content for all media within five years, according to a global survey released on May 6th, 2008 by the World Editors Forum, a subsidiary of the World Association of Newspapers (WAN).[3] All the editors in charge of a newspaper or magazine find it difficult to incorporate the online world even though they all know that the online world cannot be halted. Everything seems to be so different. Print journalism is offer-oriented, covering a diversity of topics, offers a greater degree of perception and is paid for by the reader. Online journalism is demand-oriented, more topical, quicker, more interactive and mostly for free.

In Germany, this difference has led to a number of models as to how the content is to be processed by the editorial staff – ranging from a separate online appearance with occasional texts from print editors to a print and online integration.[4] The content workflow shows experimental features: as far as the editorial aspect is concerned, for a print media brand there are neither firmly defined models of success as to which prerequisites are required for cross media distribution and establishment on the Internet. Nor are there factors of success as to how the content workflow – taking into account its individual types of distribution (print or online) – is to be carried out at optimal costs. Renate Köcher[5] says that it is a big challenge to develop intelligent integrative concepts for media markets on different platforms, whilst taking into account the specific potential of each media cate-

---

1 Cf. http://events.apple.com.edgesuite.net/1001q3f8hhr/event/index.html (as of March 8, 2010).

2 Cf. http://bit.ly/cYRmDM (as of March 8, 2010).

3 Cf. Zogby (2008), p. 6.

4 Cf. Schantin/ Juul/ Meier (2007), p. 5f.

5 Cf. http://de.wikipedia.org/wiki/Renate_K%C3%B6cher (as of March 8, 2010).

gory.[6] She adds that each category has specific talents, specific communication qualities, a fact that hasn't been considered enough. If online journalism becomes an integral part of the daily routine of the editorial staff within five years, then, in order to be fit for the future, it will only be consequent to set the degree of integration now and to adjust the editorial workflow of each morning paper to its online capacity. Furthermore, to declare the velocity of the online world the benchmark of all operational sequences, including distribution and marketing. Blogs, communities, and moving images – a morning paper cannot realize these Internet applications in print.

Its daily appearance is highly influenced by them, though. In terms of creativity, the editorial staff will have to change their print journalism in such a way that their heart will beat online. Gathering information, writing, planning and putting into operation an issue – everything has to subordinate to the dictate of the online world; in print journalism one has to adapt one's own character in order to find one's raison d'être.

1.1 The print- and Internet-related dilemma of German daily papers

Specific events such as the death of a celebrity or a momentous political decision may serve to highlight the quandary dailies have found themselves in since the advent of the Internet and the ongoing development of further digital distribution channels. Is the daily to present its layout pretending this apparently most important report is actually news to potential readers? Is it to ignore rivaling media platforms which have published the news speedier and sooner electronically? Or is it essential to take into account the circulation of the news via other information channels and, accordingly, to adapt the layout by constituting a distinctive focal point governing the selection of news? Papers need to define their new identity between the conflicting priorities of ignoring or incorporating digital news distribution channels. Is the time advantage in the communication of information (news) pitted against the paper by the electronic media complementary to the offer of a daily paper? Or is it the other way round: does a daily paper complete the supply of news previously distributed by the electronic media? The debate on this is ongoing and is led the more heatedly the lower the circulation figures of the printed media are dropping and the reach of the electronic media are increasing.[7] Often, in attempts at predicting the future relation between print and online, studies in media science refer to Riepl's Law, according to which a new medium does not so much replace the established one as assign a new

6 Cf. Köcher (2008), p. 22.

7 Cf. http://www.bdzv.de/schaubilder+M51fb47b30df.html (as of March 8, 2010).

role to it. Thus, a complementary relation is engendered.[8] A case in point is the relation between dailies and the television about 50 years ago, when, initially, dailies sought to ignore the rise of the new medium and then meant to fight it for its competition in generating advertising revenue.[9] Subsequently, not only was co-existence accepted as irrevocable but also reciprocal subsidy was viewed as an opportunity.[10] Whosoever wants to watch television, can use a daily as a TV guide. From this observation, of how two media have modified their relationship into a mutually beneficial one, there emerged the conception for a survey of print-online convergence. The present examination is a continuation of a previous study of the author, which investigated within the scope of a bachelor's thesis the possibilities newspapers have to refer in the print edition to new or additional content on the web site (qualitative approach) and how persistent they are when making use of these possibilities (quantitative approach). The examination was about institutionalized references to Internet content – something we already know from newspapers publishing TV listings. Creatively highlighted references representing a newspaper's offline link to the online world of the web are an example of it. On this basis, the online affinity of 102 German daily newspapers in print form was examined and the options for the print world to refer to the web were presented and quantitatively recorded. The gathered web references were categorized and cataloged in order to demonstrate the diversity of the web references during the sample period of April 2009. This resulted in a profile of each newspaper as to what kinds of web references it prefers. Such a profile, however, can provide information on each newspaper's online strategy and its operative implementation only to a limited extent. The present study has set as its goal to present workflow models for integrating print and online and, respectively, convergent content production. Lastly, the study wants to ascertain the status quo in Germany as represented by a survey among editors-in-chief of German newspapers. The results of the survey build the foundation for developing an evaluation method for convergence between print and online in editorial departments of daily newspapers. The starting point of the study is the model of an organizational alignment introduced by Doug Guthrie[11] to the author and based on David A. Nadler[12] and Michael L. Tushman[13]. According to their congruence model, not only the structure of an organization decides on its

---

8 Cf. Riepl (1913), p. 5f.

9 Cf. Schulze (2004), p. 35f.

10 Cf. Krell (2008), p. 27.

11 Cf. http://w4.stern.nyu.edu/faculty/facultyindex.cgi?id=348 (as of March 8, 2010).

12 Cf. http://www.nacdny.org/PDF/bio_nadler.pdf (as of March 8, 2010).

13 Cf. http://bit.ly/9P6MPU (as of March 8, 2010).

success, but also the interaction of the structure with the culture, the employees, and the task of the organization.[14] With the aid of this model the array of questions prompted by Andy Kaltenbrunner[15] et al. in their convergence model[16] is to be validated, categorized as well as extended and completed in accordance with the findings of the organizational alignment. The adjusted set of questions was to serve as a basis for a new, practice-oriented method for evaluating convergence which allows conclusions to be drawn about structure, culture, people and tasks of the editorial department in order to ascertain whether the content production for print and online is organized in a parallel, cross-medial or integrated way. For this purpose, it was necessary to conduct a survey of the newspaper industry in order to determine a guideline with the aid of benchmarks in the four single categories. This quantitative survey allows for a qualitative analysis since individual deviations from the norm indicate weak points, priorities and strong points.

The depth and quality of the analysis depend on the quality of the quantitative survey of the newspaper industry (are benchmarks representative?) as much as they depend on the quality of the set of questions (do all the answers allow conclusions to be drawn about the categories of the organizational alignments?). Subsequently, the intermediate steps of the examination are crucial for its significance. When asked about the practice-oriented topics newsroom, journalistic practice, organization of work and convergence the answers of the editors-in-chief provide hints as to the theoretical topics culture, tasks, structure and people. Each question offers three possible answers, each describing a partial aspect of the three models of convergence according to Kaltenbrunner et al. The allocation of the models of convergence to the four categories of the organizational alignment with ten questions results in a matrix describing how each model of convergence is lived in practice. A points system for evaluating the answers makes the description quantifiable and comparable.

1.2 Precise definition of the aim of the study

The aim of this study is the creation of a concept for assessing the convergence between print and online in editorial offices of newspapers. The idea is to gauge quantitatively the degree of online affinity in the German newspaper market. Not only will the status quo of forms of organization among German dailies be analyzed according to the model of organizational alignment (culture, tasks, people, structure), but also ultimately an inherent in-

---

14 Cf. Nadler/ Tushman (1997), p. 38.

15 Cf. http://www.medienhaus-wien.at/cgi-bin/page.pl?id=13 (as March 8, 2010).

16 Cf. Kaltenbrunner/ Meier/ Garcia Avilés/ Kraus/ Carvajal (2009), p. 275ff.

strument for measuring and visually representing this status quo will be developed.

To achieve this, the following central questions need to be addressed:

- Looking at the editorial offices, what is their degree of readiness to embrace the novel demands that have arisen in the wake of the emergence of the Internet and what is their willingness to regard online affinity as an investment in the future of the print world?
- What should be the job descriptions of the staff to ensure that online affinity leads to a meaningful online integration in the world of print?
- What level of training do the staff of an editorial office need to successfully achieve online integration?
- How does the editorial office need to be structured to bring the level of training of the staff to bear and to further the online affinity?

The aim of this study is the quantification of these seemingly soft factors by means of an empirical survey. The title of this contends that the heart of a daily beats online. Figuratively speaking, the analysis in hand is to provide an instrument for measuring the heart rate and then comparing it with both, the other participants and the best performers in the newspaper industry. It is with some reservations only that the findings of the survey are universal to the entirety of the newspaper industry. Universal validity, as the study will show, is subject to the input of the newspaper market under scrutiny.

1.3 Approach and structure of the research

The basis for the collection of a quantitative statistics of print and online in Germany is a survey among a total of 107 German dailies composed in the following way: 100 editors-in-chief from outside the Axel Springer AG for which the investigator is working in a senior capacity, two editors-in-chief responsible for two papers simultaneously (Aachener Zeitung/Nachrichten and Weser-Kurier/Bremer Nachrichten) as well as five papers from the Axel Springer consortium (Die Welt, Welt kompakt, Bild-Zeitung, Hamburger Abendblatt, Berliner Morgenpost). The survey began on October 16th, 2009, and finished three calendar months later, on January 16th, 2010. The selection of the papers participating was made in accordance with the convergence evaluation model as developed by Büffel (see chapter 2.4.4). To a limited degree it allows for the deduction of conclusions representative of the German newspaper market in its entirety (see chapter 5). The collection of data was necessary in order to add a quantitative dimension to the convergence evaluation model according to Kaltenbrunner et al. (see chapter 3.1). It is due to the transparency of its derivation that the data collected in the survey is considered suitable for forming the basis for the comparability of convergence as intended by the author. The limits of its significance have been sufficiently appreciated (see chapter 4.1) and expressly stated in the closing remarks (see chapter 7). Supplementary to the quantitative aspect of the convergence evaluation model there was added a qualitative dimension in accordance with the organization model of Tushman and Nadler (see chapter 3.2). As a result of this, the answers pertaining to the survey may be aligned horizontally to the three types of newsroom, as well as, vertically, to the four categories culture, tasks, structure and people as propounded by Tushman and Nadler (see chapter 3.2). By extending the matrix to comprise 40 questions there emerged a quantitatively watertight and qualitatively specifiable means of displaying individual forms of organization in newspaper production. Supported by the quantitative basis the generation of mean averages for each of the four categories of organizational alignment turned into a mathematical exercise the result of which has, at least, significance for the state of convergence of those papers participating.

By extension – always bearing in mind the limitations of the representative value – it may be indicative of the entire German newspaper industry. A means of comparability between papers was thus achieved. Any potential application of the convergence evaluation model to encompass either the entire German or any international markets is, therefore, not conditional on its fundamental functionality but, rather, on the representative meaningfulness of the data in hand. The convergence evaluation model used for this study dealt with the virtual market of the participating papers. Its functionality was reviewed by means of a qualitative consideration and analysis within the Axel Springer group of newspapers for the following three newspaper categories – street sale, local and national papers. This review was carried out in accordance with the questions governing this examination and which may be summed up as follows:

- How consciously was the degree of interconnectedness between print and online in the offices brought about? Was it masterminded?
- To which degree can convergence between print and online be masterminded at all?
- What significance is currently accorded the degree of interconnectedness, and what might be its future impact?
- Which factors of success are vital for print desks in relation to online?
- Regarding culture, tasks, structure and people, what shortcomings

are apparent today?
- What course is the form of organization likely to take in the foreseeable future?
- Is it foreseeable in which year online is going to be more important than print?

The qualitative analysis along these guiding questions in the in-depth-interviews is designed as a counterbalance to the restrictive vantage point of the multiple-choice questionnaire. As such, it is open-minded as to the answer. The interview, then, allows for the clarification and explanation of potential discrepancies between it and the underlying answers in the questionnaire. The crisis of identity, a dilemma commonly shared within the newspaper industry since the advent of the Internet, may well lead to contradictions on an operative level and is to be presented in this study as one result of the analysis. The debate surrounding the gradual emphasis and adequate pace of convergence between print and online necessarily engenders a measure of volatility regarding the implementation. As such, it was part of the motivation for this study.

Chapter 1 (Introduction) discusses the motivation for recording the convergence between print and online in the newspaper industry by means of quantitative measurement. The aim of the study is the development of a concept to analyse the degree of convergence. Moreover, the first chapter summarises the several steps carried out in the study and offers a definition of the most relevant journalistic terms used.

Chapter 2 (The state of discussion in theory and practice) discusses the technological changes and journalistic trends in the transmission of news as well as the economic and structural repercussions for the print trade since the advent of the Internet. The relevant models for the evaluation of convergence between print and online in the newspaper industry are introduced and critically examined.

Chapter 3 (Deduction of assumptions and implications for methods) draws conclusions from the current convergence evaluation models and specifically links them to organizational alignment in order to deduct the concept for a quantitatively oriented evaluation model.

Chapter 4 (Methods applied for data gathering) introduces and discusses the architecture of data gathering. The pros and cons of a survey method using multiple choice questions are critically looked at and the opportunities and limitations regarding the handling of the survey results are revealed and explained.

Chapter 5 (The results of the survey) is concerned with the presentation of the results of the survey. They are graphically enhanced in connection with organizational alignment and are clustered in such a way that they express, within limits, some significance for the German newspaper industry. Preparatory to the analysis the data is classified with a view to the constituents of organizational alignment.

Chapter 6 (Qualitative analysis of the quantitative results) applies qualitatively the graphical enhancement of the quantitative results of the survey. Analyzing three publications of the Axel Springer press by means of in-depth-interviews in order to verify the analysis instrument carries this out.

Chapter 7 (Closing remarks) summarizes and critically appreciates the results. The limits of the survey and starting points for further studies are shown up.

Chapter 8 (Bibliography) assembles the literature used for this study augmented by a list of the Internet links used.

About the use of journalistic terms

In describing convergence, two media are juxtaposed horizontally, the spheres of print and online. Terms such as "print", "(news) paper" and "offline" are used synonymously for the print domain, and "online", "Internet" and "web" for the online sector. Vertically, there is a distinction between "back end" and "front end". "Back end" denotes internal operations which are also called "workflow" and which are taking place in the "newsroom" or at the "newsdesk". "Front end" means the publishing of content on "platforms", that is, online on the Internet and offline in the paper. Regarding the back end convergence of print and online happens via the degree of cooperation in the production and distribution of content as well as via the arrangement of culture, structure, tasks and people. Conversely, at the front end convergence is achieved by means of complementary back-up, that is by various kinds of references to the other medium; in the case of print to online by web references or, conversely, by web features. "Online affinity" denotes the preparedness of a medium to refer to content offers on the Internet, for example by employing web references. The term "audience flow" is used when the audience is being led – "intermedially", between two seperate media, "intramedially", within one and the same medium. A "web reference category" conjoins typically uniform kinds of web references, whereas a "web reference catalogue" brings together comparable web reference categories. To deliver content "online" means more than to provide content to a distribution channel like a desktop PC. In a context of journalistic content, this present study defines "online" as digital distribution to devices receiving digital content in any way, for example laptops, mobile devices like smartphones, tablets, even television, navigation systems and gaming portals.

2. The state of discussion in theory and practice

The discussion on the transformation of print industry into the era of the Internet emanates from two differently motivated groups. On the one hand from forward thinkers like Jeff Jarvis[17] who, among other things, prophesied the end of print journalism in interviews, lectures and on his Internet site[18]. Jarvis urges that each newspaper publishing company should fix a date for switching off its printing machines for newspapers: "Atoms are a drag."[19] On the other hand from management and editorial office consultants like Mario Garcia[20] who helps companies that are in a process of change integrate the Internet into daily work processes. Garcia says that each employee no longer works for a newspaper but rather for a news agency serving all platforms.[21] Both requests are based on the understanding that newspaper-publishing companies turn into media companies and that the editorial offices not only print their news on paper but also spread them digitally. Newspaper publishing companies and editorial offices struggle with the change. Despite the losses in circulation[22], newspapers still earn huge profit margins. Hence the publishers do not push on with the process of change. At the same time the profit of Germany's newspaper industry has dropped to such an extent that it cannot be compensated for by profits generated through the Internet. In this context the Munich publisher Hubert Burda is often quoted who publicly said in January 2009, "You get lousy pennies on the web."[23] In its annual report 2009, the BDZV came to realize that "in the majority of cases Internet investments – despite huge growth rates in online advertising – are strategic investments which are to be cross-subsidized. The publisher's core business still remains the printed edition."[24] It is undisputed that online will catch up; the question is how long it takes. The media company Axel Springer in Berlin, for instance, has planned, according to its own account, to generate half the turnover and profit digitally by 2015. The question is how is this to be done in the future? Whereas the London quality pa-

---

17 Cf. http://www.buzzmachine.com/about-me/ (as of March 8, 2010).

18 Cf. http://www.buzzmachine.com.

19 Jarvis (2009), p. 123.

20 Cf. http://garciamedia.com/about/bio/dr_mario_r_garcia (as of March 8, 2010).

21 Cf. Garcia (2008), http://bit.ly/bEr8r9 (as of March 8, 2010).

22 According to IVW, the total circulation of German daily papers fell by 14.6 percent between 2000 and 2007.

23 Quote from Hubert Burda's speech at the DLD conference in Munich on January 25, 2009.

24 Kansky (2009), p. 5.

per Daily Telegraph can be taken as a role model for having successfully, quickly integrated and structured print and online.[25] Other papers have proceeded more cautiously. It was not until September 17, 2009 that the US quality paper Washington Post announced its intentions to integrate the paper's print and online operations.[26] The New York Times can afford to build up a research and development department in order to integrate into its journalistic work all possibilities that Internet technology offers and to open up new business areas.[27] The direction of the theory is obvious: the Internet is the future for journalism.

Jay Rosen[28] says, "the web offers huge opportunities for quality journalism."[29] In practice the dilemma becomes apparent: at present, online journalism, taken by itself, is not profitable yet. In its annual report (2009) on all 351 German daily papers, the BDZV comes to the conclusion that "newspaper publishers have failed so far to monetize online audiences sufficiently."[30] One thing is for sure: the editors adapt at different paces to the fact that the Internet will govern the future. Stephen Weichert[31], as indicated by the title of his book, provocatively asks the question: "What do we need newspapers for?"[32] The answer: It is the books that make the money. More apt is the statement in the subtitle of his book: "How the Internet revolutionizes the press." It cannot be predicted yet how long this revolution will last or whether it is an evolution rather than a revolution.

The range, measured by media analyses, makes a point as to how many readers are reached by the news supply. It has become an important, if not the important factor. Andreas Wiele, member of the management board of Axel Springer AG and head of Bild – Germany's best selling daily paper –, considers range rather than circulation as the decisive factor of success. "We don't care if it is 3.5 million printed copies or 5 million online retrievals," Wiele points out.[33]

---

25 Cf. Campbell (2008), p. 20.

26 Cf. Kramer (2009), http://bit.ly/3gzIYN (as of March 8, 2010).

27 Cf. Rogers (2006), http://www.iwantmedia.com/people/people62.html (as of March 8, 2010).

28 Cf. http://journalism.nyu.edu/faculty/rosen.html (as of March 8, 2019).

29 Rosen (2009), p. 175.

30 Kansky (2009), p. 6.

31 Cf. http://de.wikipedia.org/wiki/Stephan_Weichert (as of March 8, 2010).

32 Weichert/ Kramp/ Jakobs (2009), title of the book.

33 Wiele (2009), p. 25.

2.1 Starting position on the German newspaper market

According to the survey among American editors-in-chief in 2008, 86 percent expect that integrated newsrooms for print and online will be the norm to produce for all types of media in the future.[34] In the transitional period, newspaper companies get under financial pressure. According to its annual report, the BDZV states that the total turnover of all German newspapers (9.1 billion euros) dropped below the 1995 level (9.2 billion euros). In the same period of time, the gross domestic product in Germany rose by a third – 34.8 percent to be exact.[35] The proceeds arise from two sources, namely, distribution and advertising sales. Whereas sales revenues increased by 30 percent between 1995 and 2008 (mainly due to increase in prices), advertising revenues decreased by 21 percent. In 2008, BDZV announced that daily newspapers had registered a decrease of net advertising revenues in comparison with the previous year by 4.2 percent to 4.37 billion euros. According to BDZV, daily newspapers still hold top position as leading vehicle for advertising in Germany. A decrease by 4.2 percent stands for a reduction of revenues of approximately 185 million euros. As for online offers, net advertising revenues increased at the same time by 9.4 percent to 754 million euros in comparison with the previous year. An increase of approximately 75 million euros does not compensate for losses caused by the print sector. According to BDZV, the following economic assumptions can be resumed as follows:

- The newspaper as a print product is still strong-selling and a billion euro industry in Germany, despite years of losses.
- The daily newspapers generate additional proceeds through their online offers. Growth rates are relatively high.
- In absolute terms the increase of turnover of the online sector cannot yet compensate for losses caused by the print sector.

Apart from economic indices one can observe two contrary developments in terms of range of print and online offers. According to a survey by the Institute For Public Opinion[36], from 2000 to 2009 the range of daily newspapers dropped from 77.3 percent to 69.3 percent in the age group 30 years or older, in the age group 14–29 years the range dropped from 53.4 percent to 38.9 percent. At the same time Internet usage rose from 16 percent to 63 percent (total population), from 28 percent to 89 percent in the age group

---

34 Cf. Zogby (2008), p. 7.

35 Cf. Keller (2009), p. 31f.

36 Cf. http://www.ifd-allensbach.de/ (as of March 8, 2010).

14–29 years. Journalistic studies emphasize the importance of Riepl's Law, according to which print and online as types of media are complementing rather than replacing each other.[37] But it is obvious that if news and reports are published online the pressure of justification will increase for the newspapers – they need to be read regardless. The Internet is going to afflict the print sector rather than replace it. Due to this rather basic assumption and with regard to the stated economic aspects, newspaper companies need to answer the following questions:

- Is the business model about printing and selling paper or is it about producing and selling (or distributing) content?
- How does the daily newspaper as a media brand preserve the range economically, organizationally, structurally and journalistically during and after the transitional phase from print to online?
- How does the daily newspaper change as a product?

From a scientific point of view, there are only sparse answers to these tendentiously pragmatic questions. Prognoses on the right balance between the old and the new business model can only be made speculatively. The transition towards a multimedia brand has begun. For reasons mentioned above, the increase in range cannot be completely monetized, because new market participants like Google enter the Internet market. In 2008, the websites of the ten biggest German newspaper-publishing companies together turned over 4.8 percent of Google's turnover, which amounted to 1.7 billion euros.[38] Changes of products are mainly subject to the editorial staff and their marketing departments. Whereas with the advent of the web in 1994 science went over to explaining phenomena and impact on the media business, investigations on the development of the media business consisted only of the enumeration of case studies, which were supposed to have exemplary character[39], a string of interviews with visionaries of the business and media scientists[40], or the alignment of empirical surveys and opinions[41]. The unmistakable attempt to set up a model for the future culminates in management consultants' promises to provide pragmatic solutions to the problems. In a strategy paper of 2008, the Munich management consultancy Roland Berger points out that as for print media in the digital age "there's life in the old

---

37 Cf. Krell (2008), p. 44.

38 Cf. Kansky (2009), p. 11.

39 Cf. Pirker/ Bauer/ Buchsteiner/ Granigg (2009), p. 4ff.

40 Cf. Weichert/ Kramp/ Jakobs (2009), p. 70ff.

41 Cf. Project for Excellence in Journalism (2008).

dog yet."[42] Moreover, the consultancy states nine factors of success for the transitional phase of digitization whose essence is that newspapers are to use the strength of their brand and that they are to act as orientation aids for information seekers. It becomes obvious that Roland Berger is trying to put the market positioning of the newspaper, i. e. the product, at the center of change. This area, which can be perceived by the public, will be referred to as front end in the following investigation. The consultancy company Schickler opted for a different approach when working for WAZ Media Group in Essen.[43] In the course of digitization, the company's restructuring concept recommended an efficiency improvement in the organization of the editorial staff and of processes between the four neighboring papers that all belong to the publishing company. Along with cost-cutting measures, the content was to be published through a common Internet platform (DerWesten.de). Measures aiming at processes that change the company's internal structure and process take place at the back end. There have hardly been any scientific studies on weighting and coordination of measures taken at the front end and back ends. Kathrin Meyer made an attempt to incorporate into an ideal-typical model the fundamentals and outlook of a cross-media cooperation between print and online editorial departments of daily newspapers in Germany.[44] But her study did not go beyond conceptual status: neither has its short-term course of action nor the cross-media model of rotation for integrated editorial departments of daily newspapers gained acceptance on the newspaper market. Presumably, the model lacks evidence for practical suitability. It does not offer ways allowing the model to individually adapt to the particular markets. Studies frequently restrict themselves to stating the challenges they gained through observing phenomena and associated surveys. Mike Friedrichsen[45] names four challenges:

- Transfer of content to the Internet.
- Classical proceeds models of media companies need to be examined and adapted.
- Offline content increasingly needs to be integrated into online processes.
- Integration of user-generated content[46].

---

42 Mogg/ Franke/ Seibert/ Veer (2008), p. 1.

43 Cf. Lafrenz/ Schlankardt/ Moring (2009), http://files1.derwesten.de/pdf/Praesentation_WAZ_Betriebsversammlung_2009-03-04.pdf (as of March 8, 2010).

44 Cf. Meyer (2005), p. 312ff.

45 Cf. https://www.xing.com/profile/Mike_Friedrichsen (as of March 8, 2010).

46 According to OECD user-generated content is a media content that is created and published by end-users rather than by paid professionals and experts in the field.

"It's not about replacing classical media production (e.g. editorial departments). It's about generating added value through integration,"[47] Friedrichsen says. His view is contrary to that of Gisela Schmalz.[48] "As to the web, it is necessary to couple content with interactivity. Many media decision-makers have more difficulties in approving of this challenge and in redefining media content than online-users,"[49] Schmalz points out. In saying so, Schmalz undertakes the far-reaching attempt to causally link front end to back end:

- Media content for the Internet inevitably differs from that of daily newspapers. Classical journalists, however, often fail to make full use of it – at the back end.
- Readers as users are ready for skilful and new ways of editing media content – at the front end.

When evaluating historically the threats to newspapers, Sonja Krell[50] comes to the following conclusion: the newspaper as competitor to other forms of media has proved to be "extremely adaptable"[51] and that "one can still assume that there is a complementary relation between the newspaper and other forms of media."[52] This applies to the threats of television, radio and the Internet. The complementary connection between print and online comes into being on two levels. On the one hand, it is seen at the front end. This is the case when the newspaper also uses the news flow for its online edition, considers content offers on the Internet, or leads its readers there.

Likewise the other way round: when the Internet accepts the offer provided by the newspaper. On the other hand, it is seen at the back end. This is the case when the editorial department of a newspaper organizes the news production in such a way that the news can be spread both online and offline, i.e. working processes become adapted to the requirements of the digital world (to those at the front end as well).

---

47 Friedrichsen (2007), p. 15.

48 Cf. http://www.yeseconomy.net/?page_id=18 (as of March 8, 2010).

49 Schmalz (2009), http://bit.ly/4bch5F (as of March 8, 2010).

50 Cf. https://www.xing.com/profile/Sonja_Krell (as of March 8, 2010).

51 Krell (2008), p. 25.

52 Krell (2008), p. 51.

2.2 Fundamentals and Changes of Newspapers

The production of what daily newspapers refer to as content – i.e. the editing of information in a journalistic manner – comprises three fundamental working steps, namely, the constant gathering of information (investigation), the compiling and classifying of information in order to set up topics (selection), and the writing in order to publish.[53] Markus Anding and Thomas Hess offer a twofold definition of content.[54] According to the epistemological approach, information is regarded as raw material for human knowledge; information enriched with knowledge is depicted as content. According to the economic approach content is regarded as public property, which does not turn into private and protected property until it is being shaped editorially. Both approaches have in common that the human being as an individual occupies center stage in order to give a specific value to information or content. The human being is the link that closes the value-added chain between that what happened and the publishing of the report on that incident.

Jeff Jarvis terms this kind of newspaper production as "content economy"[55]. According to this model, the newspaper places a content offer on the market (newspaper market). The newspaper producers hope that the content will find its customers (readers). The value of content is determined by the number of readers (circulation or range). To this approach Jarvis opposes one he terms "link economy"[56], according to which the value of content is not determined by number of copies sold. It is the links that give a value to the content in the Internet. In this context linking means how often do other Internet presences refer to this particular content and lead the user to it. Technically, links are a connection between elements to a different destination on the web, activated by a mouse click. This differentiation, in the sense of a convergence theory, is important as his understanding of content includes the Internet by definition. You cannot possibly measure the value of content without the Internet – but you can do it without print. Jarvis emphasizes the radical nature of his approach not only by demanding that the end of the industry should be determined, but also by corresponding implications. Thus, he considers present production processes involving investigation, opting for a topic and its publication as obsolete. In order to meet the requirements of the link economy, the following conditions for convergence need to be fulfilled. Firstly, the value-added chain starts earlier and online. Secondly, the value-added chain ends later and online.

---

53 Cf. Gottschalk (2007), p. 220.

54 Cf. Anding/ Hess (2003), p. 8f.

55 Jarvis (2009), p. 49ff.

56 Ibidem.

Thirdly, the story, which in the past exclusively would have been published in print, still is important – it is, however, merely one link in the value-added chain (see figure 1).

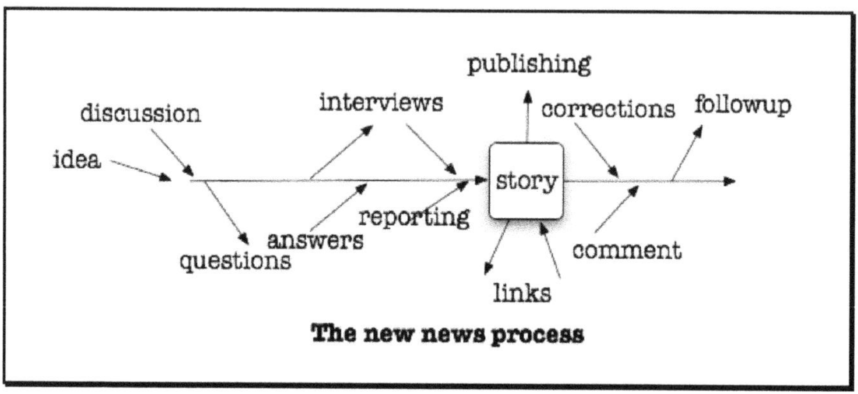

Source: Jeff Jarvis.

Figure 1: Workflow model according to Jarvis

The convergent production process (the new news process) starts with an idea and a discussion about it. The intention is to gather information through questions and answers in the classical sense and through communication with the Internet. Unlike in the case of content economy, where information is offered as a finished product, information is provided as an intermediate stage (story) for commentating and linking to online and offline.

On the one hand the intermediate stage allows for corrections since the knowledge of the content has increased. On the other hand it allows for a continuation since new connections can be discovered and presented through the link. These new connections themselves become the source of an idea. In order to integrate the Internet in this or similar form into the daily routine of an editorial office, Köcher sees a challenge in developing "intelligent, integrative concepts for various platforms,"[57] i. e. the convergence of print and Internet in the course of digitalization of the original newspaper business.

2.3 Editorial convergence between dailies and Internet

Surveys among newspaper producers, to whom editors-in-chief, their deputies and executive editors may belong, do not present a homogeneous pic-

57 Köcher (2008), p. 22.

ture of the future situation in editorial offices. This finding confirms Köcher's demand for an integrative conception for editorial offices. According to the already mentioned worldwide survey (which was conducted in 2008) among 704 people employed in print and online departments[58], 44 percent of the employees thought that news would be read online in the future. 31 percent of the respondents believed that the newspaper would still be the leading medium for news exchange. 35 percent wanted to train journalists for the new media, 31 percent deemed it appropriate to take on new journalists. 56 percent assumed that news could be read for free in the future, 33 percent believed the opposite, whereas 11 percent were undecided. The majority did not question the prediction that integrated newsrooms will become the standard form of news reporting (86 percent), that journalists agnostically work at media platforms (83 percent), and that the newsroom configuration promotes the teamwork (83 percent). As a result, on the one hand the Internet becomes an integral part of the daily routine of an editorial office, on the other hand there is no standardized, deductive instruction on how to get there. Specialist literature on this topic, of which the intention is to show individual models for the future, is internationally provided by the WAN, for the U.S. market, inter alia, by Project For Excellence in Journalism in Washington, and in Germany, for instance, by the Federation of German Newspaper Publishers (BDZV) and the Organization of German Magazine Publishers (VDZ). The literature however is confined to the description of already existing organization models. It is about an inductive derivation of the models. Since the economic success does not represent, for the reasons already mentioned, the decisive selection criterion for an organization model, soft factors play an important role when it comes to the acceptance of organization models. In its annual report the WAN presents international trends the company discovered.[59] Darmstadt-based Ifra GmbH periodically publishes consultation papers. These papers deal with the transformation of classical business models[60], presenting and discussing individual cases. The necessity of standardization when assessing the convergence of editorial offices is not only reflected in the different ways publishing companies are shaping their metamorphosis towards media companies.

Furthermore, the procedure of measuring convergence and creating comparability is not uniform either and leaves room for interpretations and speculations. In 2009, the business consultancy Schickler conducted a survey among 200 publishers, executive directors and managers of German publishing companies.[61] The survey found that 48 percent of the respondents

---

58 Cf. Zogby (2008), p. 4ff.

59 Cf. Vidal-Folch (2009), p. IV.

60 Cf. Pirker/ Bauer/ Buchsteiner/ Granigg (2009), p. 10.

61 Cf. Kahlmann (2009), p. 22.

considered the production of digital content in the supra-regional editorial department as fully integrated, 47 percent planned its introduction during the course of the next five years. Schickler's factual claim that nearly half the supra-regional editorial departments of the respondents are already equipped with a fully integrated print and online production is neither theoretically nor practically tenable. Firstly, for the newspaper business there is no binding definition of what a fully integrated print and online production is. From a scientific point of view there are just attempts at explanation leaving room for individual interpretations. Secondly, the practice has shown, as demonstrated in many case studies, that within editorial departments and publishing companies there have been serious attempts to fully integrate print and online. Cost management, missing sources of income, insufficient training, refusal attitude of editorial staff or uncertainty, however, have prevented or at least obstructed a full integration. Therefore, the compromise consists of a mixture of forms of organization, which integrate online but still put the main emphasis on print.[62]

2.4 Models of assessment for convergence in editorial departments

The development of the technologies used and the introduction of new technologies can effect dynamics in production processes and limit the tenability of assessments. These facts make it more difficult to assess the convergence in editorial departments. Models of assessment show interim findings of evolutionary processes of change, depending on method (survey, content analysis, samples), approach (description of practice or setting up of theories) as well as business model and use. For the goal of this examination the following models of assessment need to be critically appreciated.

2.4.1 Convergence evaluation according to Kaltenbrunner et al.

In 2009, Andy Kaltenbrunner, Klaus Meier, José A. Garcia Avilés, Daniela Kraus and Miguel Carvajal conducted an international comparison of daily newspapers in terms of newsroom convergence. Their study found that – from the publishing companies' point of view – the first decade of the Internet (1994–2004) was characterized by "speculative bubbles and multimedia phrases, trial and error."[63] The second decade, i. e. since 2005, has been characterized by discussions about convergence in the daily routine of an editorial department.[64] "New ways of obtaining and exploiting news in

62 Cf. Roth (2005), p. 74.

63 Kaltenbrunner/ Meier/ Garcia Avilés/ Kraus/ Carvajal (2009), p. 264.

64 Ibidem.

new structures, in newsrooms and at news desks"[65] would systematically arise. These ways, however, "have in common the intention to create centers whose task is to control the work and dataflow when aggregating and distributing digital materials. Online services as well as print media are being served from those newsrooms."[66]

On the basis of preliminary and case studies, the authors of the convergence study mentioned above classify models of newsroom convergence into three categories, which can be summarized as following:[67]

1. Full integration: the infrastructure for the editorial production of content is centrally controlled in one single newsroom in order to coordinate the workflow for all media platforms and channels in a convergent way. Convergence is strategically as well as operatively an explicit business goal, an economic and journalistic process of development. Considerably more than half the journalists work for at least two media platforms and receive appropriate training or further education.
2. Cross-media: the majority of journalists are trained for a particular media platform. Hence, it is possible to subdivide the respective newsrooms into print and online. Central and comprehensive control of the workflow and content use by coordinators and news managers form the connection between the media platforms. Team building of staff working for different platforms is possible; it is even promoted through further education. Cross-medially effective work requires that at least one fifth of the staff should be capable of working for various platforms (multi-skilling).
3. Coordination of independent platforms: there is deliberately no cooperation between various forms of media, neither as to the provision and production of news nor as to its distribution. Subsequently, convergence is not a strategic goal of the company. The company's intention is to maintain its powerful, autonomous units without risking diluting the journalistic core competences and without giving up the specific identity of the platforms. Cross-mediality at best arises from individual interest or is due to reasons of promotion.

The authors to both an underestimation and an apprehension of the Internet ascribe the varying degrees of intermedial symbiosis found at dailies.[68]

65 Kaltenbrunner/ Meier/ Garcia Avilés/ Kraus/ Carvajal (2009), p. 264.

66 Ibidem.

67 Cf. Kaltenbrunner/ Meier/ Garcia Avilés/ Kraus/ Carvajal (2009), p. 275.

68 Cf. Kaltenbrunner/ Meier/ Garcia Avilés/ Kraus/ Carvajal (2009), p. 262.

While the ones had reacted tardily to the changes brought about by the Internet, the others had alleged some form of cannibalization by the Internet, of their printed editions. Yet others, it was suggested, had embraced the net hoping for new prospects. Due to the differing response times there emerged, at editorial offices, varied degrees of convergence. By categorizing the degrees of convergence the authors created a means of comparing individual editorial offices along a common matrix using four convergence descriptors.[69] The four relevant descriptor categories are project frame within the corporation, newsroom management, journalistic practice and labor organization and human resources development. Each investigation is based on 32 questions. The analysis of samples from Germany, Spain, and Austria concluded that not a single one of the companies investigated was entirely committed either to the model of complete integration or that of cross-media or to the model of coordination of independent platforms. However, the underlying matrix might help towards an improved structuralization of strategic considerations. It could also be used to develop distinctive convergence concepts. With reference to the Convergence Continuum model[70] as postulated by Larry Dailey et al.[71] the authors consider the systematic change within news corporations to be part of an inevitable evolutionary process that is only just beginning. Recipients (the reading public), they say, are a step ahead of the media corporations in freely using all platforms available.

2.4.2 Convergence evaluation according to Schantin

Dietmar Schantin has developed convergence models for the organization of newsrooms[72] that take into consideration this evolutionary process of adjusting the medial supply to the apparently sophisticated demands of the reading public.[73] Using practice-oriented examples Schantin transferred the operating procedures into three distinct basic models:

Newsroom 1.0: Multiple-Media Newsroom: in this model its own proper editorial staff manages each platform, print and online.

Newsroom 2.0: Cross-Media Newsroom: in this version reporters and authors do not submit their contents to any particular platform but instead they assist their colleagues on the platforms.

---

69 Cf. Kaltenbrunner/ Meier/ Garcia Avilés/ Kraus/ Carvajal (2009), p. 275f.

70 Cf. Dailey/ Demo/ Spillman (2003), pp. 1f.

71 Cf. http://journalism.unr.edu/faculty-staff//app-faculty/6/larry-dailey/ (as of March 8, 2010).

72 Cf. Schantin (2009), p. 8.

73 Cf. Schantin/ Juul/ Meier (2007), p. 5f.

Newsroom 3.0: Media-Integrated Newsroom: in this case there no longer is any assignment of editorial responsibility or contents-generation to any one platform. It is exclusively the production staff that specializes in the features of the platforms (see figure 2).

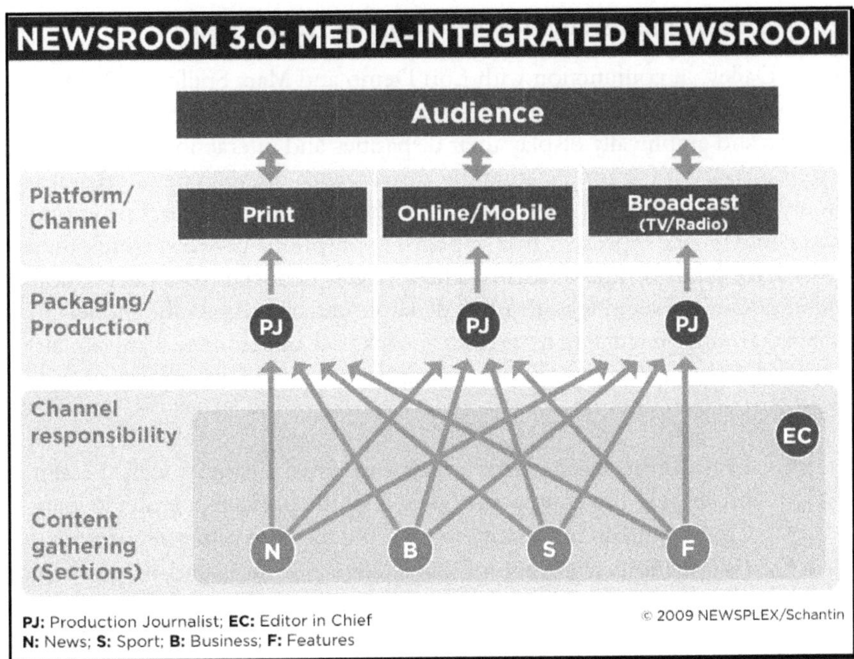

Source: Dietmar Schantin.

Figure 2: Convergence model Newsroom 3.0 according to Schantin

While he elucidates the development from the first through the third newsroom structure, Schantin sees in none of the models a solution that could be generally binding for all editorial offices. He says that "every news operation needs to find the workflows and structures that best meet its needs and the needs of the market."[74] Part and parcel of this is that staff who year in year out used to think in terms of printed papers need to develop an awareness for the online world.[75] Otherwise the evolutionary process might well end in a refusal of participation and acceptance. Accordingly, the degree of convergence depends substantially on structures, functions, staff, and corporate

74 Cf. Schantin (2009), p. 9.

75 Cf. Schantin-Williams (2007), p. 17f.

culture.[76] Just like the evaluation model according to Dailey et al. the convergence models set up by Schantin serve as an alignment for editorial offices meaning to deduce their prospective editorial organization. It would follow that his convergence models offer less of a quantitative valuation than a qualitative guideline that can continuously be updated.

2.4.3 Convergence evaluation according to Dailey et al.

Larry Dailey, in conjunction with Lori Demo and Mary Spillman (2003), used the Convergence Continuum model to try and classify convergence models and graphically display their disparities and interactions. Their model offers a concept for appreciating the convergence between news organizations, termed newsroom (see figure 3). According to them cross promotion and convergence represent two opposed conceptions between which there exist three kinds of hybrid forms. The model is deduced from the relation to other newsrooms and is tolerant of dynamic variance. Since the model is shaped around practice in newsrooms, back end and front end are similarly affected and, accordingly, are not separated in terms of classification.

- Cross Promotion: use of words and visual elements with the aim of promoting the contents produced by the partners, involving logo.
- Cloning: unaltered rendition of contents from other newsrooms.
- Coopetition: exchange of knowledge but independent production of contents in separate newsroom.
- Content Sharing: regular meetings in order to collate ideas and contents pertaining to a common topic.
- Convergence: collaborative generation of topics using the strengths of own platform to contribute to joint story.

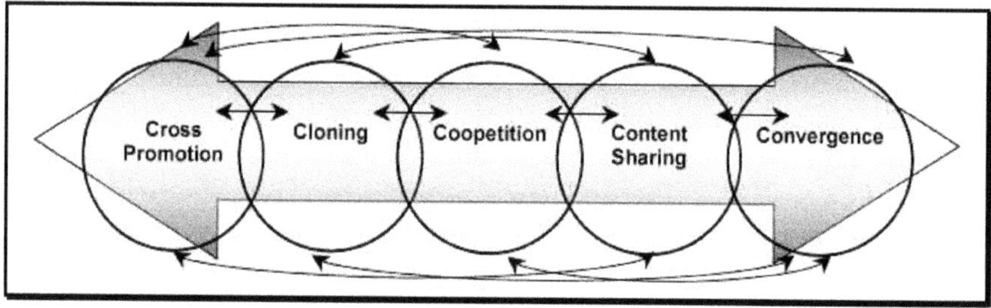

Source: Larry Dailey.

Figure 3: Convergence Continuum model according to Dailey et al.

---

76 Cf. Schantin-Williams (2007), p. 15.

The Convergence Continuum model is an instrument for describing and evaluating degrees of convergence, not for assessing convergence as such.[77]

2.4.4 Convergence evaluation according to Büffel

Given the assumption that front end recipients show an interest in content supply which "even newspaper traditionalists find it hard to escape"[78] and given, further, that there is a need for co-ordination and cooperation across the distribution channels, it is crucial to review the state of convergence in an editorial office. Whatever, for reasons historical, economical, journalistic or structural, has led to the various peculiarities of editorial convergence in the back end has repercussions for the front end. There was, for instance, the question of how the established medium (print) was to react to the new one (online), whether there should be cross-medial references from one to the other. True to the reasoning of the inevitable evolutionary process the next conscious steps in this process took stock of the status quo, not only in the back, but in the front end, too. The question was in which ways and to what degree of penetration do newspapers advertise to their online offer – and vice versa. Since 2006, Steffen Büffel, following the lead of the American Bivings Group[79], has been analyzing the online performance of the 102 largest German newspapers. He is aiming for "a status quo survey of how, in the course of time, newspapers have opened up their online offers towards Social web, thereby encouraging a dialogue between the paper and its readers, or developing video or audio formats to enhance the presentation of multi-medial contents."[80] As part of his study Zeitungen online[81], Büffel concluded for the sample period, September 2008, that by that point in time 82 percent of the newspaper websites sampled offered videos (either in-house produced or bought). The increase by 11 percent against the previous year and by 45 percent against 2006 serves to indicate the multi-medial alignment of newspapers as organized in the back end and carried out in the front end. For the purposes of the survey 20 features were defined and the presence of each paper in the Internet was counted. The ranking of German papers according to the sum total of web features[82] used in 2008 oscillated

77 Cf. Dailey/ Demo/ Spillman (2003), p. 9f.

78 Kaltenbrunner/ Meier/ Garcia Avilés/ Kraus/ Carvajal (2009), p. 288.

79 Cf. Johnson (2008), http://bit.ly/by83Bv (as of March 8, 2010).

80 Büffel (2009), http://www.media-ocean.de/forschung/ (as of March 8, 2010).

81 Cf. Büffel/ Spang (2008), http://bit.ly/9ANXZI (as of March 8, 2010).

82 In 2008, the features comprised RSS-Feed, RSS-Categories, RSS-Text, RSS-Advertisement, most viewed/ most popular stories, videos, audio-podcasts, chats, journalist blogs, commentary in journalist blogs, blogroll in journalist blogs, comments on articles, mandatory registration, social bookmarking, forum, mobile version, social networking, user generated content, geocoding, tagging.

between 14 (DerWesten.de of WAZ group) and zero as reflected in the Fränkische Landeszeitung (flz.de), the Bremen paper Weser-Kurier (weser-kurier.de and bremer-nachrichten.de) and the Nordsee-Zeitung (nordsee-zeitung.de). However, this ranking offers only limited information as to how dailies exploit the possibilities the Internet offers. Papers, which offer a small variety of features in their online version largely, use the Internet as a quantitative extension to their print contents rather than as a qualitative diversification. A year on[83], these observations were corroborated. Hardly any changes were registered. Once more the range of web features used was between 14 (WAZ group) and zero (Fränkische Landeszeitung and, this time around, Badische Neueste Nachrichten and Märkische Oderzeitung). According to Schmalz, the selection and number of web features used indicates the aspiration of the website to exploit the possibilities of the Internet. By the same token, using Büffel's evaluation scheme, the alignment of the survey can be turned around to find out with which amount of features papers integrate the Internet at the front end. Methodically, and differing from Büffel's approach, who first defines and then counts the online features, it seems judicious to begin with a qualitative inventory of offline features used by the papers. This way it should be possible to rule out any hypothetical non-consideration of features.

2.4.5 Convergence evaluation according to Haller et al.

The upgrading of technologies and the discovery of new fields of application for these technologies not only changes the environment for readers and users at the front end but also that of the content producers at the back end.[84] The acquisition of information, e.g. via Google, is simplified while, at the same time, problems are compounded regarding content distribution across several platforms. There is a heightened expectation among journalists to be able to manage all the platforms. From this, it does not inevitably follow that the quality of the journalistic product diminishes.

Accordingly, Michael Haller[85], refraining from evaluating convergence along organizational or empirical lines, approaches evaluation from the angle of quality of production. Consulting the personnel involved in the workflow convergence is assessed according to its benefit for both the product and the process of production. Haller dubs his approach "benchmarking"[86].

A benchmark he defines as a diagnostic measuring system, which uses a reference point as reference level for a measured best performance. Unlike in

83 Cf. Büffel (2009), http://www.media-ocean.de/forschung/ (as of March 8, 2010).

84 Cf. Schneider (2009), pp. 80f.

85 Cf. http://www.unileipzig.de/journalistik/haller.htm (as of March 8, 2010).

86 Cf. Haller (2004), p. 2.

business studies he does not use benchmarking as an instrument for rationalizing work, but as a market-oriented model with quantifiable characteristics that reliably measures and evaluates journalistic performance. According to polls carried out in editorial offices[87], 60 percent of respondents felt that since the introduction of the news desk communication with colleagues had increased. 86 percent of respondents observed an increase in quality of their paper. This improvement was explained by 50 percent of these respondents as originating in their greater personal share in responsibility.

2.4.6 Convergence evaluation according to Roth

In any convergence evaluation between print and online the new medium, Internet, represents the dynamic constituent which, owing to technological innovation, is subject to permanent change and thus constantly modifying its relation to print. Judith Roth[88] has analyzed this process of change identifying three distinct levels: on a micro-level there are criteria like typography and layout, on a meso-level the journalistic concept and on a macro-level the cross-linking of print and online. She finds confirmation of the mutually conditioned change in the fact that since the year 2000 most publishers of dailies have switched their journalistic concept by consolidating their online commitment.[89] This adds to convergence a strategic element which Roth does not derive from enquiries, but which she extrapolates from the product itself. By dubbing her research method autopsy she denotes an empirical variant of content analysis, the origin of which she locates in the history of journalism.[90] Roth has put forward theses concerning operative convergence, which may be summed up in the following way:

- Publishers of daily papers refer actively and passively from online to print.
- Publishers of daily papers use cross-medial links from online to print and vice versa.
- The publishers' products are linked up reciprocally and supramedially.
- The web address of the online product features in the print edition.
- Publishers of daily papers advertise their online edition in print.

---

87 Cf. Schneider (2009), p. 83.

88 Cf. http://www.kindermedienagentur.com/roth.htm (as of March 8, 2010).

89 Cf. Roth (2005), p. 74.

90 Cf. Roth (2005), p. 59.

According to Roth, the analysis of the way in which a pool of 34 dailies vie for attention with regard to their online offer serves to confirm the thesis that the newspaper market is an attention market. Its purpose is to intermedially guide the reader's attention. The convergence analyzed in the front end led to observations about the back end, such as the fact that the print editorial office is still the number one content supplier for the net, and the online areas are text-dominated. Most of the online appearances are dominated in cooperation within the journalistic unit.[91] This kind of representation only indirectly allows for a differentiation of convergence in the production of journalistic contents, for example if the journalistic concepts are categorized according to the purpose and conduct of online appearances. Current phenomena certainly necessitate the adaptation of obsolete strategies. From all this, meaningful results can be culled with some reservations only. It is, for instance, of secondary importance in the interlinking of print and online whether the web reference occurs by publisher advertisement or by editorial reference. With a view to assessing the online affinity of a paper, both ways of guiding the reader's attention towards the net are of equal efficiency: "Publishers of daily papers interlink their products."[92] In part as marketing instrument for gaining new readers, in part as reciprocal stimulation of both media. It is not shown what possibilities there are as such for bridging the gulf between print and online and with what frequency this is done. With her way of deducting strategic questions Roth represents the publishers' attitude towards changes in the online environment. The stabilizing force of a paper (e.g. its high profile, credibility etc.) apart, the convergent acting of editorial departments is not appreciated to the degree Haller accorded it with his remarks about quality in the newsroom. In saying that "there are attempts at directing the attention from the print to the online edition and vice versa"[93]. Roth concludes that initial worries for an invigorated online edition putting paid to the print trade seem to be subsiding. By contrast, the printing of so-called links makes it easier to name references for additional information.

2.4.7 Convergence evaluation according to Gottschalk

The examination approaches the online affinity of 102 German newspapers from the printed form of the news, and records the possibilities of web references used in the print world with the help of a content analysis. No distinction was made between subscription and purchase models of newspapers; neither edition nor reach was considered (and with it not the respective distribution market). Both of those aspects are irrelevant to the object of the

---

91 Cf. Roth (2005), p. 167.

92 Cf. Roth (2005), p. 158.

93 Cf. Roth (2005), p. 158.

examination. Also the format is not decisive: web references adapt themselves like photos to the size of the paper. The amount of pages of the newspapers plays a computational role in the examination period: The absolute amount of web references is to be put in relation to the total of pages to determine the relative amount of web references per page. The examination period from March 2nd to 7th, 2009 was chosen for the content analysis arbitrarily and should fulfill one condition: the fact that on six consecutive weekdays from Monday to Saturday neither a national nor a regional holiday influences the production terms. The ascertained web references were collected, categorized and listed to show the variety of the web references in the examination period. From this database a unique profile emerges for each paper as to which kinds of web references are preferred.

Prior to this examination all available material on the subject of convergence in newspaper editorial offices was evaluated from three points of view. Firstly, there is the intermedial and presumably complementary relation between print and online environment in the newspaper industry. Secondly, the process-conditioned relations between the internal work routine to produce content and the content publication on the distribution platforms. Thirdly, it was a matter about the theories and attempts at explanation of the case studies of putting up assessment models for the convergent working reality in the future. The qualitative and quantitative content analysis should deliver the reproduction of the reality of 102 well-chosen German newspapers as a basis to develop the practice-oriented computation pattern. The representation of the result of the research consists of three subdivisions. Firstly, the description of the different kinds of web references found (qualitative evaluation), then their frequency of use in each of 102 newspapers (quantitative evaluation). Finally, the relation of the amount of the web references to the amount of the pages can be expressed in ranking lists, which show how many web references each newspaper uses per page as a link from print to the Internet. The results do not just give an overview of the amount of possibilities for web references in German newspapers. The performance expressed in the ranking discloses the differences in the online affinity clearly and could become a motivation to reach a better order in the ranking lists. The interaction that happens between the work routine in the background (employees, tasks, culture, structure) and publishing in the front (distribution print and online) is indisputable after consideration of all the models for the convergence assessment. After the capture of all possibilities for web references in newspapers, a systematic counting up was carried out, in the contents analysis, of how often each single newspaper uses which kind of web reference on every single one of six days in the examination period. That has generated a matrix that lists the newspapers vertically and lists the days with the respective number of web references horizontally. From this material a ranking of the newspapers with the most web references per page could be obtained. The qualitative examination culled a total of 24 different categories of web references which can be summarized basically in three catalogues: URL addresses in five different forms, teasers in five different forms, technically advanced web references to new media and services. The counting up among 102 German newspapers proved that a total of 7608 web references were used. As a weekly average each paper used 75 web references. 39 newspapers, that are 38 percent of the total number examined, were above this average in their use of web references.

Of the total of 7608 web references 94 percent (7156) can be subsumed in four categories: a simple URL address and URL address with slash word, a simple Teaser and Teaser with slash word. The categories belong to the web reference catalogues URL addresses and teaser. Of the third web reference catalogue, termed technically demanding web references, 185 web references were counted, which conforms to 2.43 percent of the total count. With 14 out of 24 categories, the third web reference catalogue is normally the biggest one of all three. On average per paper/week 19 out of 24 web reference categories never appeared once. Two of the 24 web reference categories were used in each case only just once: RSS-Feed and chat.

The total of how many web references were used in each issue of a newspaper can provide only limited information on the online affinity of the editorial staff. The possibility for the placing of a web reference decisively depends on the available space in an issue. During the examination period 7608 ascertained web references appeared in a total of 25800 newspaper pages. While in absolute consideration the average value lay as a benchmark with 75 web references per week (with six dates of publication), this figure is put into perspective when considering the references per page. Therefore, on average 0.3 web references appeared per newspaper page. This conforms to one web reference per 3.39 pages. 37 newspapers lay above average – 36.3 percent of the newspapers. On average the newspapers with the highest online affinity employed between 0.8 and 0.7 web references per newspaper page. On account of the different conditions which are largely due to the number of pages available, the relative consideration of the web reference use offers a more precise assessment of the online affinity of the newspapers: The relative consideration provides information on the number of references per page instead of per edition and will here be referred to as Q (T) in this study. The quotient of the total of web references used and the amount of pages is calculated in the following way:

$$\text{web reference quotient } Q\,(T) = \frac{\text{Total of web references } (T)}{\text{Total of pages } (T)}$$

Abendzeitung Munich published on average 0.8 web references per newspaper page (in absolute terms a total of 247 web references across the week) and achieved the highest web reference quotient Q (T). The lowest web reference quotient was 0.06 (Märkische Oderzeitung had a total of nine web references on 160 newspaper pages) as against an average quotient of 0.3 web references per page. The newspaper Bild had 96 web references on 126 pages and was second in the ranking with Q (T) of 0.76.

The ranking according to the quantity or frequency of the use of web references obviously disregards an important factor: the qualitative variety of the web references used. Although Abendzeitung Munich considered only three different kinds of web references, it booked the top rank with a web reference quotient Q (T) of 0.80. It would appear that creativity, then, is not mandatory in this ranking. For a more meaningful statement about the creative link between print and online, another component needs to supplement the web reference quotient Q (T). This component would reflect the variety of references used. This way some differentiation can be made between newspapers that publish web references, but do not underline their online affinity with an own web site. If the total of web reference categories is termed k and is followed by 1 for offering a web site, the multiplication with the web reference quotient Q (T) proves the web reference factor F_k (Q) that is constructed by the following mathematical equation:

$$\text{web reference factor } F_k (Q) = (1 + k) \times \frac{\text{Total of web references (T)}}{\text{Total of pages (T)}}$$

According to this formula, the web reference factor for the newspaper Bild amounts, for example, to F_7 (0,76) = 6.08. That means: the newspaper Bild has used seven web reference categories in the investigation period and on an average 0.76 web references per newspaper page. The product result of 6.08 produces the comparability with other newspapers, irrespective of whether other newspapers have used more web reference categories or more web references per page. Compared with the ranking by the help of the web reference quotients Q (T), the qualitative component is stressed by the ranking of the web reference factor F_k (Q). The new ranking takes the second main focus into account and makes a huge difference. The explanatory power of the second analysis instrument exposes Abendzeitung Munich: With Q (T) still on the top rank, its web reference factor F_3 (0,80) = to 3.20 is lower than that of another 14 newspapers; they showed more variety and consequently a bigger creativity to steer the reader on the Internet. The average value of the web reference categories used by 102 German newspapers amounts to 3.64. That means: only newspapers that have used at least four web reference categories are better than the mean average. Of 55 newspapers that have used a broad variety of web reference categories in this area, 26 newspapers lie with the F_k (Q) under the industry average of 1.53. Obviously, there is an imbalance here between creativity (variety of use) and penetration (total number of references used per week). Just vice versa: Though in six newspapers with an above average F_k (Q) the frequency of web references is high, but not the variety of their categories – in these six newspapers the k value is less than 3.64. The industry-average newspaper shows a web reference factor of rounded up F_4 (0,3) = 1.53. This means that a newspaper on average offers a web reference on every three pages and should aim at using four different web reference categories a week. The records of the industry lie with web reference factors of F_7 (0,76) = 6.08 and F_8 (0,60) = 5.40. The examination of the 102 largest daily newspapers showed these results by taking into account that convergence differs:

- Qualitatively, 24 different web reference categories of three web reference catalogs were discovered in the newspapers.
- Quantitatively, the average newspaper used 75 web references per week; the highest number was 247.
- Relative to the number of pages the newspapers used 0.3 web references per page; the highest number was 0.8 web references.
- On average the newspapers used 4 web reference categories per week; the highest number was 8.
- Comparability is possible of newspapers and to benchmarks with two calculation models: focusing on quantity (penetration) via ranking according to web reference quotient Q (T) and, in addition, focusing on quality (i.e. variety, creativity) through ranking according to the web reference factor F_k (Q).

The strengths of both calculation models Q (T) and F_k (Q) for audience flow from print to online can be summarized in this way:

- Understandable and checkable comparability of the online affinity of the own newspaper to the industry with the help of the web references.
- New clues as to the measurement and acceleration for the change management by the convergence development with the Internet.
- Another use is as a means for an assessment of the balance between qualitative and quantitative approaches.

3. Deduction of assumptions and implications for methods

Recapitulating the approaches discussed above, three dimensions of convergence can be determined concerning the evolutionary process of the inter-medial symbiosis of print and online:

- The degree of convergence, the weighting ratio between print and online as undertaken both strategically and operationally in the back end.
- The time frame of convergence, when a gradual shift from print to online takes place, both in the back and the front end.
- Visibility of convergence, the way the front end inter-medially refers to the other content offer.

According to Jarvis the interplay between the workflow in the back end (staff, job description, culture, structure) and the act of publishing in the front end (print and online distribution) is beyond controversy. Simply by dint of the dissimilarity of the respective properties of the two media, the complementary fusion of print and online makes for an extension of both reach (quantitative approach) and presentation of contents and brands (qualitative approach). To achieve this a finely tuned workflow in the back end is essential. A workflow in which three convergence models form categories (complete integration, cross-media and platform difference). Haller acknowledged the benefits of fine-tuned workflow at the news desk in his benchmark target when analyzing the workflow in various editorial departments.[94] For the editorial side he made out an improvement in quality of the paper while on the publisher's side he saw a reduction of costs through synergy effects. Schantin translated the practice into abstract organizational models of how newsrooms and workflow are structured in the various editorial departments. By means of these models he meant to facilitate the deductive derivation of individual solutions. This comprises, over and above the stipulation of some structure, a precise job description for the staff and the planning in the back end of the process of change. In his analysis the question remained unacknowledged whether by workflow adjustment in the back end and its concomitant increase in quality the potential for improvement in the front end is exhausted. In other words, whether the one medium advertises the strengths of the other. Intramedially this kind of sup-

---

94 Cf. Schneider (2009), p. 82.

port is well known. Typically it starts on the title page of a daily with a reference to an article in the inner section. The equivalent in television is the so-called audience flow. Intermedially, however, this question remains a moot point. At the very least it has not yet been exhaustively addressed. If, accordingly, there are two distinct aspects to convergence, back end and front end, then the analysis concentrates on the complementary relation between print and online at the front end. What needs clarifying is the term audience flow.

In television, audience flow[95] expresses in percent which amount of viewers of a given program continue to watch the ensuing one. In order to prevent loss of viewers to competitors TV channels use trailers to keep up the audience flow. Television-wise, in addition to the intramedial audience flow, we may observe attempts at intermedial audience flow when reference is made in news program to the respective online news portals. With regard to newspapers the intermedial audience flow is extant; however, it has not been comprehensively studied along the lines of the combination of qualitative facilities and quantitative penetration. Unlike in television, this study of intermedial audience flow in daily papers does not aim at gauging the success rate of each web reference nor on which workflow (convergence model) the complementary relation (see figure 4) is based.

The models so far introduced for the evaluation of convergence between print and online are either quantitative or allow for conclusions to be drawn about the categories of convergence. In this context, Büffel and Roth are rather front end-oriented, while Haller, Kaltenbrunner et al. and, in particular, Schantin and Dailey et al., put the emphasis on the back end. None of these evaluation models, not even the autopsy method applied by Roth, is aimed at the definition of qualitative attributes, which might be accorded benchmark status by way of an empirically comprehensible content analysis.

Haller's analysis reflects an opinion rather than offering comparability of individual papers along an industrial standard or benchmark. Aiming to redress this imbalance the study run by Gottschalk strove to develop a model for the front end of daily papers in terms of diversity (quality) and penetration (quantity) that defines touchstones and establishes commensurability. The study in hand continues the work for serving the audience by creating a measurement system for the back end of a newspaper company (workflow), but needs to be seen in a broader context as follows.

95 Cf. Mahrdt (2008), http://bit.ly/4tieOe (as of March 8, 2010).

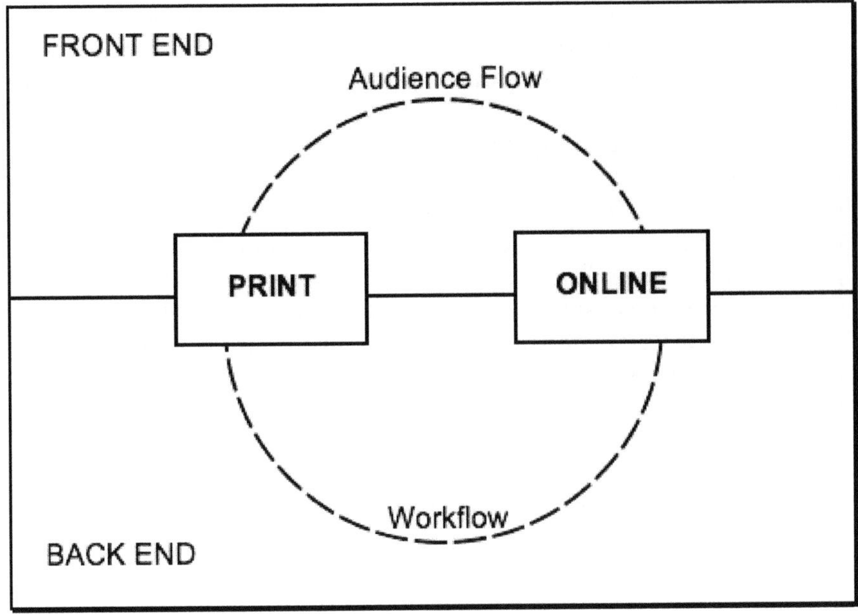

Source: Pit Gottschalk.

Figure 4: Complementary relation of print and online

3.1 Assumption of three types of newsroom

Following Kaltenbrunner et al. and Schantin, the study presupposes the existence of three types of newsroom. In order to set up the multiple-choice questionnaire the definitions need to be summarized (see chapters 3.1.1 and 3.1.2). Subsequently, the attributes of the three types need to be assigned to the questions. The current survey assumes the following underlying definitions of newsroom types.

3.1.1 Isolated or parallel newsrooms

In terms of an online-first principle in the editorial office, online is not being favored. The senior journalist of the corresponding platform decides autonomously. It might lead to a competition between the various platforms, because the senior journalists of the various platforms govern the news flow independently as each platform works independently. Various journalists bear responsibility for the corresponding platform, but each platform has its own editor/editors in charge and the editorial conferences will be held separately. It may be the case that individual journalists are appointed to act as comprehensive interface. The cooperation with other platforms is being promoted little and often even regarded as problematic. Most commonly there are various Content Management Systems (CMS), since there is no need for a permanent data exchange. Research, production and distribution remained and remain as it used to be – adjusted to the needs of the respective platform. Technical multimedia equipment for research is not available for each journalist. The sourcing happens for each department autonomously. Technical equipment at the production level is not available for all journalists, either. Also technical equipment at the distribution level is not available for each journalist; it is not foreseen. Research for a platform takes place irrespective of material requirements of other platforms, and the platforms are independent of each other. Journalists specialized in print media do not need to consider technologies and processes of online, radio or TV distribution. Experience with the various platforms is the exception, not the rule. It is the result of personal interests of individual journalists rather than obligation. So, experience with the various platforms is not necessary even for news production or distribution. Just 0 – 20 percent is the share of multi-skilled journalists in the editorial. Video production is possible, inhouse and by a third party, depending on the costs. The qualification for spreading reports to other platforms via Facebook, Twitter or other social media applications is neither necessary nor required. It is possible, but not the rule that print journalists influence or control the coverage of the online edition.

It is rather not the case that the coverage of the online edition influences the print journalists. Each platform is anxious to preserve its idiosyncratic character. There is a kind of rivalry between the online and print platforms, when it comes to covering the best stories. If it is necessary to alter archived or linked online articles, these alterations will be prompted by the online platform, mostly out of self-interest. It is rather not the case that the journalists chat online and systematically with their readers about their coverage. And the distance between the newsrooms is of no importance. There are various newsrooms or editorial offices that are separated from one another. So, the staff have a negative attitude towards the introduction of only one newsroom; print and online are to work separately. Without further actions, there will be more disadvantages than advantages. It is feared that the quality of each media platform will decrease. The number of employees remains the same. Separating the platforms does not change anything. If it turns out the competitors' concepts of convergence are more successful, it might lead to reduction in staff due to cost concerns. The participation on advanced training programs is only occasionally being promoted. There is only personal motivation for multi-skilling and even different cultures on each platform. The basic understanding as to journalistic work may differ substantially on both platforms in order to deliberately avoid a blending of methods and a standardization (passing on) of attitudes towards journalism.

The introduction of convergence would create no new professional roles. It is rather the exception that journalists offer and run their own blogs independently of the newsroom. Convergence at the level of the enterprise might be one possibility – it does not take place in the newsroom. Convergence is neither a compulsory goal of the company nor a tool. Convergence at the level of the enterprise might offer a promising outlook for the future – but only at that level. If the introduction of convergence is put into practice, it is mainly the result of initiatives taken by individual employees.

The cooperation of journalists is done of their own accord, and is promoted (and aimed) by departmental managers. Talks about the strategies were held exclusively at the level of the management. Change management is not necessary. Journalists maintain their work routine. Each individual platform even has its own IT-specialists – for print and online. The platform of the first publication is decisive. The contents are optimized for the platforms.

3.1.2 Cross-media newsrooms

In terms of an online-first principle in the editorial office, cross-media editors decide case-by-case which strategy is to be applied. Both online-first and the strategy to withhold information exclusively for the use of the printed media are options. There is an office for print and an office for online (and possibly radio or television). Both offices are linked up instead of governing the news flow independently. Responsible news editors for each platform and comprehensive multi-media coordinators are in charge of coordinating the news. Journalists of all platforms can attend the editorial conferences. The senior editor for multimedia coordination is obliged to participate. The cooperation with other platforms is being promoted only partly – particularly, if the coordinator sets up teams. In some cases there is only one Content Management System (CMS), but usually there are various CMSs.

Only the coordinators have to use every CMS. Research, production and distribution are not separated when making stories, at least not more so than in the past. Technical multimedia equipment for research is partly available for each journalist, for instance, only some departments, not all, have their own video equipment. Only platform specialists and coordinators have access to all systems. Elaborate software is reserved for specialists. Lending of technical equipment at the distribution level is possible. Multi-skilling is being promoted. Advanced training is a possibility, but no obligation.

Multi-skilling is no prerequisite for journalists involved in the processes of news production and making of newspapers. Specializations are regarded indispensable for a high-quality production. As a result, multi-skilling is of importance only for a part of the staff. To some extent, multi-skilling is a prerequisite at the level of news distribution. It is compulsory for senior journalists or coordinators. This knowledge, however, is also helpful for all the other journalists. For research, experience with the various platforms is a prerequisite to a certain extent. It is important for coordinators who are in charge of a platform. Experience with the various platforms is helpful for news production, too. In terms of distribution of news, experience with the various platforms is only compulsory for coordinators who co-decide which channel information and reports will be published on. This knowledge would also be helpful for senior journalists, though. 20 – 70 percent is the share of multi-skilled journalists in the editorial team, i.e. journalists who are capable of working on several platforms. Video production is produced in-house or manufactured by a third party, but an own department is favored.

After consulting with colleagues of other platforms and possibly with assistance, all journalists on the move are able to spread preliminary reports via Facebook, Twitter or other social media applications. Print journalists can influence or control the coverage of the online edition, because their input is asked for and it will be considered ad hoc. The online edition increasingly attracts attention and increasingly influences the coverage of the printed edition, but not systematically yet. The story in a newspaper gains more importance through the accompanying online coverage and is therefore regarded as central. Between the platforms there is an exchange of information regarding changes that might affect the online archive, e.g. deleting outdated or false news. The journalists chat online and systematically with their readers about their coverage only case-by-case. The newsrooms or editorial offices, in which the print and online departments are run, are accommodated in the same building or at least in buildings not too far apart. There are various newsrooms that are connected (e.g. by news desks). Sometimes there is only one newsroom that is, however, divided into various sectors. Many journalists are skeptical to the introduction of only one newsroom because they fear that working conditions will worsen (more work) or that they might lose privileges. Coordinators seem to be the only beneficiaries. The number of employees remains the same. Particularly at the beginning of the process the demand for additional journalists who are experienced in the field of multimedia production might go up. Some are needed for converting material. The company offers advanced training courses to enable a better understanding of the convergence method – but just for a part of the employees, mainly designed for decision makers from cross-media coordination and technicians rather than journalists. Journalists often get paid for working for the other platforms. Between the platforms, there are different cultures, but the necessity to cooperate and to communicate leads to slow changes in terms of attitude and strategy between online and print. The brand image keeps the departments together. Coordinators for the various platforms can be recruited from higher qualified employees. Mostly, however, additional staff and knowledge is required. Journalists are free to offer and run their own blogs independently of the newsroom, after consulting with colleagues of other platforms. Convergence takes place at the level of the enterprise or at the level of the newsrooms in the editorial department or at both levels. Convergence is just a tool and a long-term process for each department separately. Thus, the introduction of convergence could be put into practice at the bottom of the hierarchy or ordered from above. The coordination often takes place cross-medially at the second or third level of management. New ideas and tests grow out of editorial practical experience. To a certain extent strategies and goals have been communicated – the employees concerned have been informed (e.g. those who are in charge of the various platforms). The technical support team is trained to be in charge of all platforms or the support is confined to one platform; both are possible. The platform is more important than a convergence strategy. The strategic distribution of various channels, however, is being taken into consideration.

3.1.3 Integrated newsroom

In terms of an online-first principle in the editorial office, the decision in favor of online-first has been made due to strategic reasons. This rule always applies. Very often online-first is regarded as a logical first step towards a convergent production structure. The news flow is centrally controlled. A centralized news editor, e.g. as head of the news division or as duty editor, is in charge of coordinating the news. All senior journalists of all platforms participate in the editorial meeting. Especially at strategic planning the number of participants is high. The cooperation with other platforms is an integral part of the editorial procedures. There is a Content Management System (CMS) for all platforms; in case there are various CMSs, there are at least interfaces for data transfer. Division of work would be a possibility if enough staff members were on hand. But print and online live on the fact that each staff member is able to carry out each working step of research, production and distribution. Technical multimedia equipment for research is available for each journalist; for instance, each department has its own video equipment. Technical equipment at the production level is available for all journalists, too. All journalists can use all systems and software, even though the organization of the editorial work is predominantly based on the division of labor. Also technical equipment at the distribution level is available for each journalist, as a matter of fact, it is accessible and available for everybody, however, in everyday practise it is used by specialists only (e.g. to edit video productions). Multi-skilling is being promoted and means that the member of the staff masters online and print. It does not mean, however, that these skills are permanently required or applied. Multi-skilling is a prerequisite for journalists involved in the processes of news production and making of newspapers. All journalists should be capable of creating content for all channels. This is the strategic goal. Multi-skilling is a prerequisite at the level of news distribution, too. To decide which is the ideal form of coverage for the respective platform is considered a basic skill of a journalist. Also experience with the various platforms is a prerequisite for research. It is important for all decisions as to how the gathered information is to be used optimally later. Even experience with the various platforms is a prerequisite for news production to a certain extent. In the news production process there are always specializations. The journalists should be at least capable of operating all platforms, though. All journalists should be able to decide how, when, and on what platform information and reports are to be published. 70–100 percent of the editorial team are capable of working on several platforms, print and online. Videos are usually produced almost exclusively in-house. And all journalists on the move are able to spread preliminary reports via Facebook, Twitter or other social media applications, depending on the decision as to how the topic is to be spread best. Print journalists can influence or control the coverage of the online edition; at the best they are themselves involved and responsible for what is written. The coverage of the online edition influences the print journalists; for the printed edition they are always looking for a new way to tackle a specific topic since they know that the story is published online. The story published in a newspaper can be considered as a highlight due to the medium of print. In the chain of publications it is, however, considered merely as a subset in a context with online.

Creating and maintaining digital contents is taken for granted and belongs to the duties as does the willingness to communicate with an online community does. The newsrooms or editorial offices, in which the print and online departments are run, are accommodated in the same building or in different buildings; it is a prerequisite that they are in the same building – there is just one newsroom. In terms of convergence in the same newsroom, the journalists are carefully prepared for the changes. It has a positive effect on job satisfaction – changes are interpreted as a chance rather than a burden. Well-equipped newsrooms are taken as a symbol. In some concepts convergence is taken as a chance to abolish jobs. More frequently it leads to changes in qualifications (and staff) rather than number of journalists. On a permanent basis for all employees, the company offers advanced training courses to enable a better understanding of the convergence method, both company internal (including training and external experts) and company external programs (participation in programs run by external institutions). There are no benefits at all, but the job prospects are significantly higher. There is a common basic understanding as to journalistic work (journalistic culture) across all platforms. There is one culture. The constant integration of all areas and all platforms also promotes a convergent journalistic understanding. Goals, target groups and (ethical) rules are being defined collectively. The introduction of convergence creates new professional roles, particularly at the levels of management (in terms of the editorial department and the enterprise as a whole) new fields of activity arise in order to bring together print and online. Editorially, this creates new tasks of communication and coordination for team leaders. Journalists are free to offer and run their own blogs independently of the newsroom on a voluntary basis – it is even hoped for. Convergence takes place at the level of the enterprise and at the level of the newsrooms in the editorial department, according to a well-coordinated concept. Convergence is both a business goal and a superior guideline/strategy. Convergence is a long-term process for the entire enterprise and hence for each single department. Thus, the introduction of convergence is put into practice from above, because convergence is understood as a superior business strategy. The whole staff from all levels of the hierarchy are systematically integrated into this process. The convergence strategies have to be communicated and discussed with the employees. Change management has been implemented. The team is trained to be in charge of all platforms. The strategic distribution of content and the question as to where this content is most efficient are of the highest importance.

3.2 Organizational alignment

According to Guthrie, the organizational alignment comprises the four components culture, tasks, structure (formal organizations) and people and rests on tenets brought forward by David Nadler and Michael L. Tushman.[96]

In their model the input of environment and resources within the context of company history governs the interior life of an organization in such a way that the components of the organization align themselves along the strategy. Given proper leadership and implementation the output in the system, units, and the individual staff member is that evident that it, in turn, has an impact on the environment and resources and so, by extension, on the input itself (see figure 5).

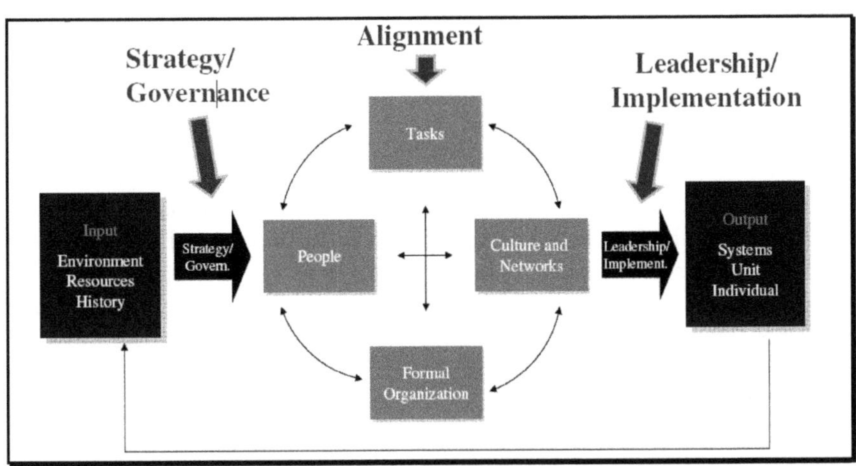

Source: David Nadler and Michael L. Tushman.

96 Cf. Nadler/ Tushman (1997), p. 28ff.

Figure 5: Organizational alignment

According to this model organizational alignment assumes a central and crucial role in a company when it comes to profitably incorporating the internal strengths and weaknesses (resources) in order to meet the challenges of competition (environment) related to the tradition of the company (history). This study will take a closer look at the set-up of the four components of alignment in order to pursue the question of how the papers adjust to post – digitization selling conditions as outlined in chapter 2. The analyzing instrument used for highlighting the preparedness for convergence in the editorial offices will have to ensure comparability of the components. Based on the assumptions Nadler and Tushman explain as a transformation process, the four components can be summarized as following in the chapters 3.2.1 to 3.2.4.[97]

3.2.1 Culture

Via the architecture of structure a company possesses culture as an informal form of organization. According to Nadler and Tushman this comprises those values, thought patterns and accepted behavior patterns of the staff that are not formally controlled. The culture has an immediate bearing on the effectiveness of the formal processes. Nadler and Tushman also call the culture "the informal organization."[98]

3.2.2 Tasks

Part and parcel of this is a systematic order of jobs and activities within the company to flesh out the structure and make its performance verifiable. Ideally the jobs and activities are in a beneficial relation to the knowledge, competence and abilities of the workforce, thus creating a culture that fills a structure with life. Nadler and Tushman also call the tasks "the work".[99]

3.2.3 Structure

The term structure, according to Nadler and Tushman, means the form of organization which, within a company, determines not only the structures and procedures but also the leadership and remunerative systems. The meaning of the term "organization" is often reduced to the architecture of structure, thus, according to Guthrie, leading to an inaccurate conception of leadership.[100] Therefore, consideration of all the aspects of alignment is cru-

---

97 Cf. Nadler/ Tushman (1997), p. 32.

98 Ibidem.

99 Cf. Nadler/ Tushman (1997), p. 32.

100 Lecture at Berlin School of Creative Leadership, class 3, on Nov. 10, 2008.

cial for a basic understanding of how a company organises its sustainability. Nadler and Tushman also call the structure "the formal organizational arrangements."[101]

3.2.4 People

Like the other aspects of alignment, culture as such is interrelated with the staff. According to Nadler and Tushman, their knowledge, competence and abilities, along with their needs and wishes, have to come into effect in an organization in order to put into practice a strategy with the desired output.

101 Cf. Nadler/ Tushman (1997), p. 32.

4. Methods applied for data gathering

The present examination has set as its goal to ascertain the status quo in the newsrooms of German daily newspapers according to the categories culture, tasks, structure, and people. The object was to develop from it an analysis instrument for assessing the degree of convergence between print and online. By conducting a survey among editors-in-chief, we ask those decision makers of a newspaper company for information who are responsible for the newsroom and hence substantially control the four categories mentioned above. The questionnaire of the survey extends the matrix model proposed by Kaltenbrunner et al.[102] in such a way that ten questions relate to each of the four categories.

4.1 Architecture of the survey among editors-in-chief

In the first step, as is the case with Kaltenbrunner et al, the assessment is carried out by means of the multiple choice format. Each answer describes one of the three types of newsrooms and its form of convergence (integrated, cross-medial or isolated). Superficially, the 40 questions deal with the topics newsroom management, journalistic practice, work organization, and convergence in general. As mentioned above, the questions used for assessment and analysis are, unlike Kaltenbrunner et al, assigned to the categories culture, tasks, structure and people – a fact which is not obvious to the respondent. According to Schantin[103], it can be observed that the types of newsrooms develop from parallel via cross-medial to integrated. In the second step, each possible answer is assigned to a particular number of points in order to make the answers of the survey quantifiable: 0 for parallel, 1 for cross-medial, 2 for integrated. Consequently, in the matrix a fully integrated editorial office would score 20 points each in the categories culture, tasks, structure and people. Editorial departments that purely work cross-medially would hence score 10 points each in the four categories. In the third step, the average value scored in each of the four categories culture, tasks, structure and people provides information as to what extent, on average, German newspaper departments are integrated. With this benchmark, newspapers can individually be compared in order to locate deficiencies or competitive advantages within the individual organizations. The quantitative aspect serves as a basis for the qualitative examination that offers a profound analysis on the basis of the individual answers.

---

[102] Cf. chapter 2.4.1.

[103] Cf. chapter 2.4.2.

4.1.1 Selection of survey respondents

According to BDZV, 351 newspapers with a total circulation of 19.95 million copies were published in 2009. 94.9 percent of which are local and regional papers (a total of 333), 2.8 percent are national papers (10), and 2.3 percent are street sale papers (8). Sunday and weekly papers do not fall in the scope of the study. In order to build a numerically solid foundation, the editors-in-chief of 107 daily papers, more than the amount defined by Büffel[104], were asked to participate in this survey. Most of them had already served as basis for the convergence model according to Gottschalk (see chapter 2.4.7.). The classes of newspapers selected for the purpose of this study deviate slightly (in percent) in terms of composition: 87.9 percent represent local and regional papers (94), 5.6 percent national papers (6), and another 6.5 percent street sale papers (7). The selected newspapers are the following supra-regional papers (in alphabetical order):

- Aachener Nachrichten www.an-online.de
- Aachener Zeitung www.az-web.de
- Abendzeitung www.abendzeitung.de
- Allgäuer Zeitung www.all-in.de
- Allgemeine Zeitung www.allgemeine-zeitung.de
- Augsburger Allg. Zeitung www.augsburger-allgemeine.de
- B.Z. Berlin www.bz-berlin.de
- Badische Neueste www.bnn.de
- Badische Zeitung www.badischezeitung.de
- Berliner Kurier www.berlinonline.de/berliner-kurier
- Berliner Morgenpost www.morgenpost.de
- Berliner Zeitung www.berlinonline.de/berliner-zeitung
- Bild www.bild.de
- Braunschweiger Zeitung www.newsclick.de
- Bremer Nachrichten www.bremer-nachrichten.de

104 Cf. chapter 2.4.4.

- Darmstädter Echo www.echo-online.de
- Der Neue Tag www.derneuetag.de
- Der Tagesspiegel www.tagesspiegel.de
- Die Glocke www.die-glocke.de
- Die Rheinpfalz www.rheinpfalz.de
- die tageszeitung www.taz.de
- Die Welt www.welt.de
- Donaukurier www.donaukurier.de
- Esslinger Zeitung www.ez-online.de
- Frankenpost www.frankenpost.de
- Frankfurter Allg. Zeitung www.faz.net
- Frankfurter Neue Presse www.rhein-main.net
- Frankfurter Rundschau www.fr-online.de
- Fränkische Landeszeitung www.flz.de
- Fränkischer Tag www.fraenkischer-tag.de
- Freie Presse www.freiepresse.de
- Fuldaer Zeitung www.fuldaerzeitung.de
- General-Anzeiger www.general-anzeiger-bonn.de
- Gießener Allgemeine www.giessener-allgemeine.de
- Göttinger Tageblatt www.goettinger-tageblatt.de
- Hamburger Abendblatt www.abendblatt.de
- Hamburger Morgenpost www.mopo.de
- Hannoversche Allgemeine gwww.haz.de
- Heilbronner Stimme www.stimme.de
- Hess./Niedersächsische www.hna.de
- Hildesheimer Allg. Zeitung www.hildesheimer-allgemeine.de
- Kieler Nachrichten www.kn-online.de
- Kölner Express www.express.de
- Kölner Stadt-Anzeiger www.ksta.de

- Kölnische Rundschau www.rundschau-online.de
- Landshuter Zeitung www.idowa.de
- Lausitzer Rundschau www.lr-online.de
- Leipziger Volkszeitung www.lvz.de
- Lippische Landeszeitung www.lz-online.de
- Lübecker Nachrichten www.ln-online.de
- Ludwigsburger Kreisz. www.ludwigsburger-kreiszeitung.de
- Magdeburger Volksstimme www.volksstimme.de
- Main Post www.mainpost.de
- Main-Echo www.main-echo.de
- Mannheimer Morgen www.morgenweb.de
- Märkische Allgemeine www.maerkischeallgemeine.de
- Märkische Oderzeitung www.maerkischeoderzeitung.de
- Mittelbadische Presse www.baden-online.de
- Mittelbayrische Zeitung www.mittelbayrische.de
- Mitteldeutsche Zeitung www.mz-web.de
- Münchner Merkur www.merkur-online.de
- Neue Osnabrücker Zeitung www.neue-oz.de
- Neue Presse (Hannover) www.neuepresse.de
- NRZ www.derwesten.de
- Neue Westfälische www.nw-news.de
- Neuß-Grevenbroicher www.ngz-online.de
- Nordbayerischer Kurier www.nordbayerischer-kurier.de
- Norddeutsche Rundschau www.shz.de
- Nordkurier www.nordkurier.de
- Nordsee-Zeitung www.nordsee-zeitung.de
- Nordwest-Zeitung www.nwz-online.de
- Nürnberger Nachrichten www.nn-online.de

- Oberbayrisches Volksblatt www.ovb-online.de
- Offenbach Post www.op-online.de
- Ostsee Zeitung www.ostsee-zeitung.de
- Passauer Neue Presse www.pnp.de
- Pforzheimer Zeitung www.pz-news.de
- Recklinghäuser Zeitung www.recklinghaeuser-zeitung.de
- Reutlinger General-Anz. www.gea.de
- Rhein-Neckar-Zeitung www.rnz.de
- Rhein-Zeitung www.rhein-zeitung.de
- Rheinische Post www.rp-online.de
- Ruhr Nachrichten www.ruhrnachrichten.de
- Saarbrücker Zeitung www.saarbruecker-zeitung.de
- Sächsische Zeitung www.sz-online.de
- Schwäbische Zeitung www.szon.de
- Schwäbisches Tagblatt www.tagblatt.de
- Schwarzwälder Bote www.sw-online.de
- Schweriner Volkszeitung www.svz.de
- Siegener Zeitung www.siegener-zeitung.de
- Stuttgarter Nachrichten www.stuttgarter-nachrichten.de
- Stuttgarter Zeitung www.stuttgarter-zeitung.de
- Süddeutsche Zeitung www.sueddeutsche.de
- Südkurier www.suedkurier.de
- Südwest Presse www.swp.de
- Trierischer Volksfreund www.volksfreund.de
- TZ München www.tz-online.de
- Waiblinger Kreiszeitung www.waiblinger-kreiszeitung.de
- Welt kompakt www.welt-kompakt.de
- Weser Kurier www.weser-kurier.de
- Westdeutsche Allg. Zeitung www.derwesten.de

- Westdeutsche Zeitung www.wz-newsline.de
- Westfalen-Blatt www.westfalen-blatt.de
- Westfälische Nachrichten www.westfälische-nachrichten.de
- Westfälischer Anzeiger www.wa-online.de
- Wiesbadener Kurier www.wiesbadener-kurier.de
- Wiesbadener Tagblatt www.wiesbadener-tagblatt.de

This results in a matrix whose y-axis represents the selected newspapers and whose x-axis represents the number of points – 0, 1, or 2 – assigned to each of the 40 questions. If a question is not answered respectively not answered completely, the mean value 1 will be used for the calculation for the time being. Those cases are marked, indicating that the answer of this particular question can be error-prone and consequently might have an effect on the result in this particular category. The possible error rate has to be taken into consideration when analyzing and eventually assessing individual newspapers in comparison with the branch average.

4.1.2 Critical reflection on the data gathering applied

When balancing pros and cons to decide which approach to adopt – the profound case based analysis or the universality of the findings – the method applied offers a balance between the rather quantitative approach of a survey and the qualitative approach of the subsequent case based analysis of daily newspapers. Bearing in mind that the objective of the study is to develop an analysis instrument, the interaction of the two steps of quantitative and qualitative data gathering offers an unique insight into an editorial office of a newspaper in the context of the industry. The limits of such a data gathering should always be kept in mind, though. The first and the second step of the data gathering involve the answering of a questionnaire that, based on the studies of Kaltenbrunner et al. and Schantin, is about describing newsroom models. The questions are set in the multiple-choice style. Depending on the respective newsroom model, the answers are awarded points. For the purpose of the analysis, the answers are assigned to the four categories of organizational alignment, which are culture, tasks, structure and people. The points of this method can be summarized as follows:

- Quantification of typical features of a newsroom according to three models.
- Profound differentiation within categories of forms of organization.
- Enables the comparability of different forms of organizations.

The weak points lie in the survey as an instrument. Firstly, the number of respondents determines the relevance of the findings. Secondly, you have to assume that the respondents answer the questions honestly and seriously. This requires that the answers offered reflect the facts of the three types of newsrooms properly. The composition of the classes of newspapers may deviate just slightly from the total stock of the German newspaper landscape; the deviation of about 6 percentage points, however, is undisputed and needs to be considered. Weak points of the data gathering can be summarized as follows:

- Reliability of editors-in chief's answers is indeterminable.
- Inaccuracy in describing the newsrooms.
- Deviation of survey objects from the industry by 6.7 percentage points.

The attempt to describe the three popular types of newsrooms by means of 40 answers is accompanied by the attempt to come up with a definition of newsroom. At present, the newspaper industry lacks a universally applicable definition, which the present study requires. The contradiction to the suggested answers along with the overdue debate on defining how the form of organization in a newsroom might look like and how it is to be described would quicken the approximation towards a universal applicability of such a profound definition. The chances of the applied data gathering method can be summarized as follows:

- Agreement on a universally applicable definition for newspaper organizations.
- Driving force for further scientific investigations of newsrooms.
- Investigations of reciprocal relations between newsroom structures and newsroom culture respectively tasks of employees.
- Assessment of future viability of existing forms of organizations, also in the sense of print and online.

The survey examines three different types of newspapers: tabloids (street sales), local and national papers. The benchmark, which is deduced from the average, could give rise to contradiction if one type of newspaper rejects the influence of another type of newspaper on the benchmark. If this is the case, then the data material needs to be differentiated. A possible danger of the multiple choice format is that the suggested attributes of the given answers do not completely or at least satisfyingly describe the individual newsroom model. In this case, missing out an answer or double answering is possible. This needs to be considered when carrying out the assessment. It has to be mentioned here that the decision as to which questions are to be allocated to the individual components of the organizational alignment is made arbitrarily and can be questioned. Still, the answer itself allows for a conclusion to be drawn about the form of organization. The risks of the applied data gathering method can be summarized as follows:

- Doubts about the derivation of industry benchmarks.
- Flawed or incomplete answers to individual questions might be produced due to a different interpretation of the term newsroom.
- Doubts about the allocation of questions to the organizational alignment.

The set-up of the questionnaire with its possible answers according to the multiple-choice format is illustrated in appendix 1 of this study. The questionnaire has been supplemented with a personal judgment by the editor-in-chief surveyed as to his own role and his conception of convergence within the scope of the editorial form of organization.

4.2 Handling the survey results

In order to achieve a meaningful analysis of the survey results, the answers rendered need to be sufficiently generated by way of the following forms of display.

- Allocation of the questions to the various aspects of organizational alignment.
- Conversion into percent of the points system of the survey.
- Visualization, by means of an adequate form of diagram, of the survey results according to the terms of reference of organizational alignment.

The advantages and disadvantages adhering to the handling of the data gathered both quantatively and qualitatively will be discussed at some length in chapter 4.1.2. First and foremost, the forms of display chosen serve to visualize correlations so as to achieve comparability of the results. This does not inherently preclude future enhancement of the forms of display.

4.2.1 Various aspects of organizational alignment

As described in chapter 3.2, organizational alignment according to Nadler and Tushman is based on the four aspects culture, tasks, structure and people. Ten each of the forty questions of the survey represent one aspect; however, they were randomly allocated to a category in the questionnaire[105] in order to avoid conclusions being drawn.[106]

The questions on organizational alignment were allocated as follows:

- Culture: questions 5, 22, 27, 31, 34 through 38 and 40.
- Tasks: questions 1, 2 20, 21, 23, 24, 29, 32, 33 and 39.
- Structure: questions 3, 4, 6 through 10, 18, 25 and 26.
- People: questions 11 through 17, 19, 28 and 30.

In each case the answers possible are based on the three types of newsroom.[107]

4.2.2 Percental representation of the results

Three possible answers were suggested for each of the ten questions governing the four aspects of organizational alignment. In the points system chosen[108] each answer is allocated a maximum of 2 points, totaling 80 points altogether. Accordingly, the points scored in the four sets of 10 questions need to be added up and multiplied by a factor of 1.25 (=100/80), in order to be expressive of the degree of maximum convergence of print and online, here termed CTSP. In terms mathematical the calculation of the degree of convergence, CTSP (Z), may be expressed in the following way:

$$\text{Degree of convergence CTSP (Z)} = \frac{C(Z) + T(Z) + S(Z) + P(Z)}{80} \times 100$$

$$\text{or CTSP (Z)} = [\ C(Z) + T(Z) + S(Z) + P(Z)\ ] \times 1{,}25$$

---

105 The categories are "newsroom", "journalistic practice", "working organization", and "convergence".

106 Original list of questions comprising the survey can be gleaned from chapter 5.1 and appendices 1 and 2.

107 Cf. chapter 3.1.

108 Cf. chapter 4.1.

Z means the number of papers selected for the average value. CTSP is an acronym of the four aspects of organizational alignment. The convergence degree CTSP (Z) shows by percent the degree of collaboration between print and online, starting at 0 percent, when there is no kind of collaboration, and fully integrated at 100 percent (see figure 6).

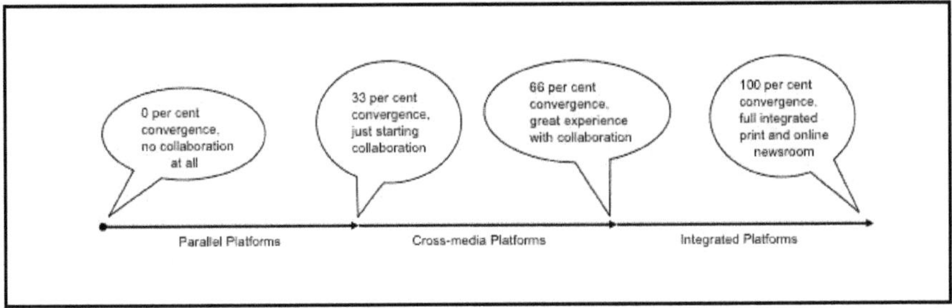

Source: Pit Gottschalk.

Figure 6: Measurement for CTSP-degree according to Gottschalk

4.2.3 Graphical representation of the results

The degree of convergence, CTSP (Z), is expressive of how closely the mean average of selected papers approaches the ideal state of the integrated newsroom. According to Kaltenbrunner et al. and Schantin, the classification of convergence, in itself, makes an important statement about online affinity in the newsroom.[109] Yet, expressing the status quo in percentages alone hardly allows for any conclusions to be made about the strengths and weaknesses of the respective forms of organization and, by extension, hardly offers any starting point for the improvement and development of convergence. The graphical representation of the poll rating reflects the composition of the result prior to percental conversion. To achieve this the number of points determined will be marked on one of four axes, each representing one of the four aspects of organizational alignment and ranging from 0 points to 20 (see figure 7).

[109] Cf. chapter 2.4.1 and 2.4.2.

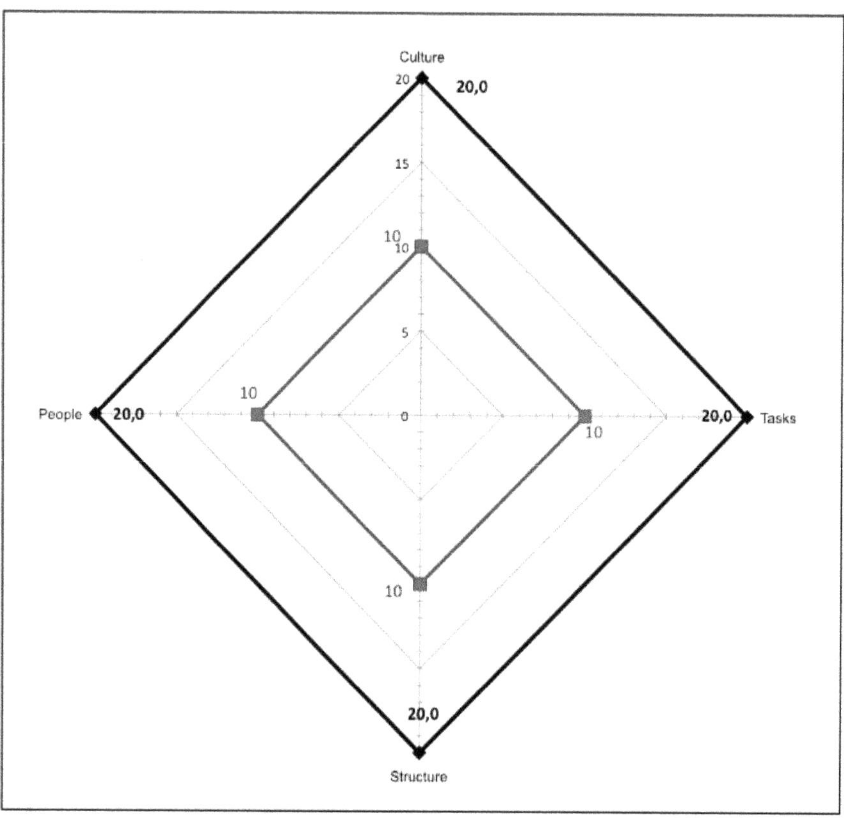

Source: Pit Gottschalk.

Figure 7: Measurable alignment according to Gottschalk

Thus, the ideal case of a fully integrated newsroom would be reflected by the outermost marking (bold black line), representing the maximum of four times 20 points while the theoretical cross – medial newsroom model would be marked by the red line. The zero point would therefore indicate non-existence of convergence. It is anticipated that there will be no case in which all four aspects are identical. Variation of the weighting ratio in organizational alignment may have its origin in either the conception or the completion of the questionnaire[110] and needs to be allowed for in any individual consideration of answers. Given the number of questions per aspect, a general drift will become apparent, anyway, and this may be revised or confirmed, if required, through individual consideration.

[110] Cf. chapter 4.1.2.

4.3 Methodical classification

The method of the present study follows two steps in order to balance profoundness and generalizability of a survey (see figure 8). The first step is about a quantitatively conclusive approach and – within the branch – a wide-ranging survey, which at least provides a random sample of the German newspaper industry. It can be assumed that the message is only representative to a limited extent. In the second step, the rather universally valid survey is deepened by a qualitative consideration of individual cases. Content-related feedback checks the validity of the questionnaire randomly.

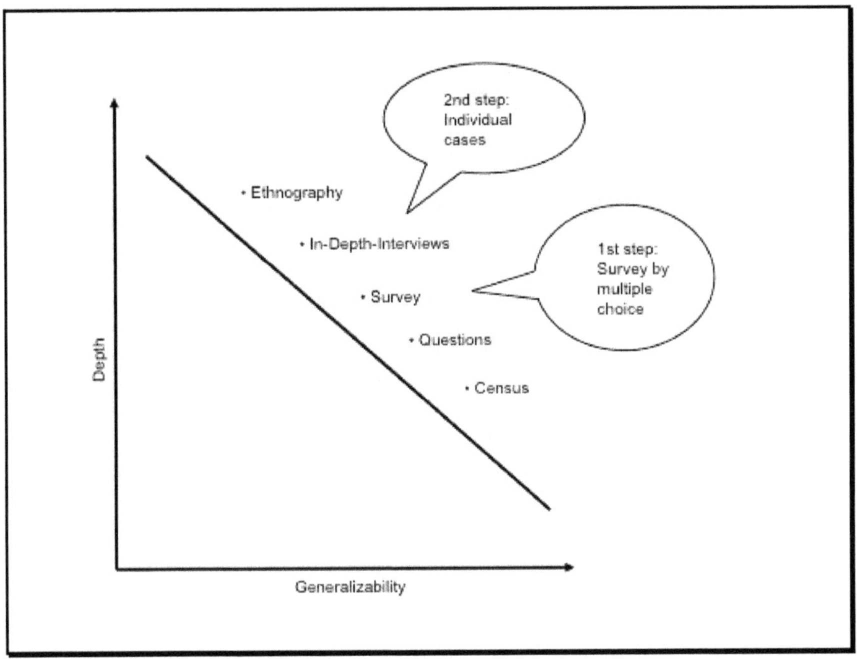

Source: Doug Guthrie.

Figure 8: Systematic data gathering

The questionnaire was sent to the editors-in-chief of 107 German daily newspapers by fax and additionally by email. It was agreed to preserve the anonymity of the respondents when publishing the survey, not, however, when processing the data.

5. The results of the survey

Out of the editors-in-chief who had been written to, 59 participated in the survey – two of whom were in charge of more than one daily newspaper (Aachener Nachrichten/Zeitung and Weser-Kurier/Bremer Nachrichten). The questionnaire was sent on October 16, 2009. The first response arrived on the very same day, the last one on January 11, 2010. The response rate amounts to 57.8 percent (see table 1). The 59 respondents represent the German newspaper industry and the 107 German newspapers, which had been written to, as follows:

Type of newspaper	Branch		Requested		Participation	
Street sale	8	2,3 %	7	6,5 %	5	8,5 %
Regional / Local	333	94,9 %	94	87,9 %	51	86,4 %
National	10	2,8 %	6	5,9 %	3	5,1 %

Source: BDZV/Schütz 2009; own survey.

Table 1: Ratio of respondents to German newspaper industry

Even though the 59 respondents as a whole represent the German newspaper industry only to a limited extent (therefore, the results of the survey are not considered to be representative), the sample provides a steady status quo of convergence of print and online in German publishing companies due to the response rate of almost 60 percent. Of a total of 2360 answers, 30 were either missing or ambiguous (more than one answer). For the purpose of calculating the convergence assessment, the mean value 1 is used for the time being, leading arithmetically to an error rate of 1.27 percent. In the data sheet (see appendix VII) the assumed mean value 1 was highlighted in gray for the purpose of identification.

As to the itemized list of results for each question (see chapter 5.1), the possible error rate within the set of 59 answers to each question was shown in such a way that the theoretical fluctuation margin becomes evident, if the assumed mean value had been 0 or 2 rather than 1. This makes clear a relativity of the individual answers to the 40 questions. With the aid of the data sheet, the answers of the editors-in-chief might indicate possible tricky conditions in a newsroom. Confidentiality allows for a description of individual results only within the scope of this study, but not publicly.

5.1 The individual answers on the questionnaire

The results for each of the 40 questions of the survey among German newspapers are listed in the same order as they were on the questionnaire, which was sent to the editors-in-chief (see appendix I). For reasons of clarity, the results were numbered consecutively and clustered into the following four categories: newsroom management, journalistic practice, working organization and convergence. The brackets in each question indicate which component of the organizational alignment (see chapter 4.2.1) each question belongs to. Based on this, the description and analysis of the survey results are prepared within the planned objective of the research.

5.1.1 Newsroom management

Question 1 (Tasks) – Is there an online-first principle in the editorial office? Or is the exclusive information reserved for the printed product? Or does not exist a clearly defined guideline on how to proceed in this regard?

- 20,3 % say: The decision in favor of "online-first" has been made due to strategic reasons. This rule always applies. Very often online-first is regarded as a logical first step towards a convergent production structure.
- 66,1 % say: Cross-media editors decide case-by-case which strategy is to be applied. Both online-first and the strategy to withhold information exclusively for the use of the printed media are options.
- 13,6 % say: Online is not being favored. The senior journalist of the corresponding platform decides autonomously. It might lead to a competition between the various platforms.

Question 2 (Tasks) – Is the news flow for print and online centrally controlled or do the senior journalists of the various platforms govern the news flow independently?

- 37,3 % say: The news flow is centrally controlled.
- 52,5 % say: There is an office for print and an office for online (and possibly radio or television). Both offices are linked up.
- 10,2 % say: Each platform works independently. Various journalists bear responsibility for their respective platform.
- Possible error of +/- 1,7 %.

Question 3 (Structure) – Who is in charge of coordinating the news?

- 39,0 % say: A centralized news editor, e.g. as head of news division or as duty editor.
- 49,2 % say: Responsible news editors for each platform and comprehensive multi-media coordinators.
- 11,9 % say: Each platform has its own editor/editors in charge.

Question 4 (Structure) – Do print and online editors both participate in the editorial meeting or does each platform have its own meeting?

- 66,1 % say: All senior journalists of all platforms participate. Especially at strategic plannings the number of participants is high.
- 27,1 % say: Journalists of all platforms can attend the editorial conferences. The senior editor for multimedia coordination is obliged to participate.
- 6,8 % say: The editorial conferences will be held separately. It may be the case that individual journalists are appointed to act as comprehensive interface.

Question 5 (Culture) – Is the cooperation with other platforms being promoted?

- 81,4 % say: Yes, cooperation is an integral part of the editorial procedures.
- 15,3 % say: Only partly – particularly if the coordinator sets up teams.
- 3,4 % say: Little. Is often even regarded as problematic.

Question 6 (Structure) – As to the Content Management System (CMS): is there a CMS for all platforms or do various CMSs for each platform exist?

- 67,8 % say: One CMS. In the case there are being various CMSs, there are at least interfaces for data transfer.
- 22,0 % say: In some cases there is only one CMS, but usually there are various CMSs. Only the coordinators have to use every CMS.
- 10,2 % say: Most commonly there are various CMSs since there is no need for a permanent data exchange.

5.1.2 Journalistic practice

Question 7 (Structure) – Research, production and distribution – are these items separated when making stories?

- 42,4 % say: Division of work would be a possibility if enough staff members were on hand. But print and online live on the fact that each staff member is able to carry out each working step.
- 27,1 % say: As a matter of fact, no. Or, to be precise: not more than in the past.
- 30,5 % say: No, it remained and remains as it used to be – adjusted to the needs of the respective platform.
- Possible error of +/- 5,1 %.

Question 8 (Structure) – Technical multimedia equipment for research: is it available for each journalist?

- 18,6 % say: Yes, for instance, each department has its own video equipment.
- 61,0 % say: Partly – for instance, only some departments, not all, have their own video equipment.
- 20,3 % say: No. The sourcing happens for each department autonomously.

Question 9 (Structure) – Technical equipment at the production level: is it available for all journalists?

- 67,8 % say: Yes, all journalists can use all systems and software, even though the organization of the editorial work is predominantly based on the division of labor.
- 25,4 % say: No, only platform specialists and coordinators have access to all systems. Elaborate software is reserved for specialists.
- 6,8 % say: No.

Question 10 (Structure) – Technical equipment at the distribution level: Is it available for each journalist?

- 59,3 % say: Yes, as a matter of fact, it is accessible and available for everybody. In everyday life, however, just specialists use it (e.g. to edit video productions).

- 28,8 % say: No, but lending is possible.
- 11,9 % say: No, it is not intended.
- Possible error of +/- 3,4 %.

Question 11 (People) – Multi-skilling means that the member of the staff masters online and print. Is multi-skilling a prerequisite for research? Should all journalists for all platforms be capable of gathering material?

- 55,9 % say: Yes, multi-skilling is being promoted. It doesn't mean, however, that these skills are permanently required or applied.
- 32,2 % say: Partly. Multi-skilling is being promoted. Advanced training is a possibility but no obligation.
- 11,9 % say: Research for a platform takes place irrespective of material requirements of other platforms.

Question 12 (People) – Is multi-skilling a prerequisite for journalists involved in the processes of news production and making of newspapers? Should all journalists be capable of creating contents for all channels?

- 67,8 % say: Yes, this is the strategic goal. Nonetheless, in the everyday execution of tasks specialization still exists in many cases.
- 27,1 % say: No. Specializations are regarded indispensable for a high-quality production. As a result, multi-skilling is of importance only for a part of the staff.
- 5,1 % say: No.

Question 13 (People) – Is multi-skilling a prerequisite at the level of news distribution? Should all journalists be able to take into account the respective distribution?

- 40,7 % say: Yes, to decide which is the ideal form of coverage for the respective platform is considered a basic skill of a journalist.
- 49,2 % says: To some extent. It is compulsory for senior journalists or coordinators. This knowledge, however, is also helpful for all the other journalists.
- 10,2 % say: No, the platforms are independent of each other. Journalists specialized in print media do not need to consider technologies and processes of online, radio or TV distribution.

Question 14 (People) – Is experience with the various platforms a prerequisite for research?

- 33,9 % say: Yes, it is important for all decisions as to how the gathered information is to be used optimally later.
- 59,3 % say: Yes, to a certain extent. It is important for coordinators who are in charge of a platform.
- 6,8 % say: No, this is the exception, not the rule. It is the result of personal interests of individual journalists rather than obligation.

Question 15 (People) – Is experience with the various platforms a prerequisite for news production?

- 61,0 % say: Yes, to a certain extent. In the news production process there are always specializations. The journalists should be at least capable of operating all platforms, though.
- 33,9 % say: No, but experience is helpful.
- 5,1 % say: No, it is not necessary.

Question 16 (People) – Is experience with the various platforms a prerequisite for the spread and distribution of news via printed means or over the Internet?

- 28,8 % say: Yes, all journalists should be able to decide how, when, and on what platform information and reports are to be published.
- 61,0 % say: It is only compulsory for coordinators who co-decide which channel information and reports will be published on. This knowledge would also be helpful for senior journalists, though.
- 10,2 % say: No.

Question 17 (People) – In your editorial team how high is the share of "multi-skilled journalists", i.e. journalists who are capable of working on several platforms – print and online?

- 15,3 % say: 70 – 100 percent.
- 61,0 % say: 20 – 70 percent.
- 23,7 % say: 0 – 20 percent.

Question 18 (Structure) – As to online videos: are your videos usually produced in-house or manufactured by a third party?

- 33,9 % say: Almost exclusively in-house.
- 33,9 % say: Both are possible, but we favor an own department.
- 32,2 % say: Both are possible, depending on the costs.
- Possible error of +/- 5,1 %.

Question 19 (People) – Are all journalists on the move able to spread preliminary reports via Facebook, Twitter or other social media applications?

- 13,6 % say: Yes. Needless to say, depending on the decision as to how the topic is to be spread best.
- 64,4 % say: Yes, after consulting with colleagues of other platforms and possibly with assistance.
- 22,0 % say: The qualification for spreading reports to other platforms is not necessary and required.
- Possible error of +/- 10,1 %.

Question 20 (Tasks) – Can print journalists influence or control the coverage of the online edition?

- 47,5 % say: Yes, at the best they are themselves involved and responsible for what is written.
- 44,1 % say: Yes, input is asked for and it will be considered ad hoc.
- 8,5 % say: It is possible, but not the rule.

Question 21 (Tasks) – Does the coverage of the online edition influence the print journalists?

- 18,6 % say: Yes. For the printed edition they are always looking for a new way to tackle a specific topic since they know that the story is published online.
- 69,5 % say: The online edition increasingly attracts attention and increasingly influences the coverage of the printed edition, but not systematically yet.
- 11,9 % say: This is rather not the case. Each platform is anxious to preserve its idiosyncratic character.
- Possible error of +/- 1,7 %.

Question 22 (Culture) – Working on a story that is to be printed – is it regarded as the pinnacle of journalistic activity or as intermediate step for coverage divided into print and online?

- 39,0 % say: The story published in a newspaper can be considered as a highlight due to the medium of print. In the chain of publications it is, however, considered merely as a subset in a context with online.
- 55,9 % say: The story in a newspaper gains more importance through the accompanying online coverage and is therefore regarded as central.
- 5,1 % say: There is a kind of rivalry between the online and print platforms when it comes to cover the best stories.
- Possible error of +/- 3,4 %.

Question 23 (Tasks) – Does the journalist or some other employee have to make sure that printed texts are to be stored in an online archive and that these texts, if new facts emerge, are to be corrected, supplemented or linked?

- 27,1 % say: Creating and maintaining digital contents is taken for granted and belongs to the duties.
- 35,6 % say: Between the platforms there is an exchange of information regarding changes that might affect the online archive, e.g. deleting outdated or false news.
- 37,3 % say: If it is necessary to alter archived or linked online articles, these alterations will be prompted by the online platform, mostly out of self-interest.

Question 24 (Tasks) – Do the journalists chat online and systematically with their readers about their coverage?

- 13,6 % say: The willingness to communicate with an online community belongs to the duties.
- 50,8 % say: Only case-by-case.
- 35,6 % say: This is rather not the case.

5.1.3 Working organization

Question 25 (Structure) – Are the newsrooms or editorial offices, in which the print and online departments are run, accommodated in the same building or in different buildings?

- 86,4 % say: It is a prerequisite that they are in the same building.
- 8,5 % say: Either in the same building or at least in buildings not too far apart.
- 5,1 % say: The distance between the newsrooms is of no importance.

Question 26 (Structure) – Are there various newsrooms or one?

- 69,5 % say: One.
- 15,3 % say: There are various newsrooms that are connected. (e.g. by news desks). Sometimes there is only one newsroom that is, however, divided into various sectors.
- 15,3 % say: Various newsrooms or editorial offices that are separated from one another.

Question 27 (Culture) – As to the attitude to work of journalists, how do they react to the convergent method?

- 57,6 % say: They are carefully prepared for the changes. It has a positive effect on job satisfaction – changes are interpreted as a chance rather than a burden. Well-equipped newsrooms are taken as a symbol.
- 39,0 % say: Many journalists are skeptical to the introduction of only one newsroom because they fear that working conditions will worsen (more work) or that they might lose privileges. Coordinators seem to be the only beneficiaries.
- 3,4 % say: The staff have a negative attitude towards the introduction of only one newsroom; print and online are to work separately. Without further actions, there will be more disadvantages than advantages. It is feared that the quality of each media platform will decrease.
- Possible error of +/- 3,4 %.

Question 28 (People) – The convergent method means that both online and print are considered when publishing. Does the convergent method have an effect on the number of employees?

- 27,1 % say: In some concepts convergence is taken as a chance to abolish jobs. More frequently it leads to changes in qualifications (and staff) rather than number of journalists.
- 67,8 % say: The number of employees remains the same. Particularly at the beginning of the process the demand for additional journalists who are experienced in the field of multimedia production might go up. Some are needed for converting material.
- 5,1 % say: The number remains the same. Separating the platforms does not change anything. If it turns out the competitors' concepts of convergence are more successful, it might lead to reduction in staff due to cost concerns.
- Possible error of +/- 1,7 %.

Question 29 (Tasks) – Does the company offer advanced training courses to enable a better understanding of the convergence method?

- 52,5 % say: Yes, on a permanent basis for all employees – both company internal (including training and external experts) and company external programs (participation on programs run by external institutions).
- 23,7 % say: Yes, for a part of the employees, mainly designed for decision makers from cross-media coordination and technicians rather than journalists.
- 23,7 % say: The participation on those advanced training programs is only occasionally being promoted.
- Possible error of +/- 1,7 %.

Question 30 (People) – Is there a cash incentive for multi-skilling?

- 37,3 % say: No, there are no benefits at all, but the job prospects are significantly higher.
- 5,1 % say: No, but journalists often get paid for working for the other platforms.
- 57,6 % say: No, only personal motivation.
- Possible error of +/- 3,4 %.

Question 31 (Culture) – Is there a common basic understanding as to journalistic work (journalistic culture) across all platforms or does each platform have its own culture?

- 45,8 % say: One culture. The constant integration of all areas and all platforms also promotes a convergent journalistic understanding. Goals, target groups and (ethical) rules are being defined collectively.
- 45,8 % say: Different cultures, but the necessity to cooperate and to communicate leads to slow changes in terms of attitude and strategy between online and print. The brand image keeps the departments together.
- 8,5 % say: Different cultures. The basic understanding as to journalistic work may differ substantially on both platforms in order to deliberately avoid a blending of methods and a standardization (passing on) of attitudes towards journalism.

Question 32 (Tasks) – Does the introduction of convergence create new professional roles?

- 54,2 % say: Yes, particularly at the levels of management (in terms of the editorial department and the enterprise as a whole) new fields of activity arise in order to bring together print and online. Editorially, this creates new tasks of communication and coordination for team leaders.
- 28,8 % say: Yes, coordinators for the various platforms can be recruited from higher qualified employees. Mostly, however, additional staff and knowledge is required.
- 16,9 % say: No.
- Possible error of +/- 3,4 %.

Question 33 (Tasks) – Are journalists free to offer and run their own blogs independently of the newsroom?

- 42,4 % say: Yes, on a voluntary basis – it is even hoped for.
- 16,9 % say: Yes, after consulting with colleagues of other platforms.
- 40,7 % say: This is rather the exception.

5.1.4 Convergence

Question 34 (Culture) – Does convergence take place at the level of the enterprise, at the level of the newsrooms in the editorial department or at both levels?

- 32,2 % say: At both levels according to a well-coordinated concept.
- 59,3 % say: Both are possible.
- 8,5 % say: Convergence at the level of the enterprise is one possibility – it does not take place in the newsroom.

Question 35 (Culture) – Is convergence a compulsory goal of the company or is it just a tool?

- 59,3 % say: It is both a business goal and a superior guideline/strategy.
- 33,9 % say: A tool.
- 6,8 % say: Neither.
- Possible error of +/- 1,7 %.

Question 36 (Culture) – Is convergence a short-term or a long-term means?

- 83,1 % say: A long-term process for the entire enterprise and hence for each single department.
- 11,9 % say: A long-term process for each department separately.
- 5,1 % say: Convergence at the level of the enterprise might offer a promising outlook for the future – but only at that level.

Question 37 (Culture) – The introduction of convergence: put into practice at the bottom of the hierarchy or ordered from above?

- 18,6 % say: From above, because convergence is understood as a superior business strategy. The whole staff from all levels of the hierarchy are systematically integrated into this process.
- 78,0 % say: Both are possible. The coordination often takes place cross-medially at the second or third level of the management. New ideas and tests grow out of editorial practical experience.
- 3,4 % say: If so, it is mainly the result of initiatives taken by individual employees. The cooperation of journalists is done of their own accord, and is promoted (and aimed for) by departmental managers.

Question 38 (Culture) – Have the convergence plans been discussed with journalists? Has change management been implemented?

- 33,9 % say: The convergence strategies have been communicated and discussed with employees. Change management has been implemented.
- 59,3 % say: To a certain extent strategies and goals have been communicated – the employees concerned have been informed (e.g. those who are in charge of the various platforms).
- 6,8 % say: Talks about the strategies were held exclusively at the level of the management. Change management is not necessary. Journalists maintain their work routine.
- Possible error of +/- 3,4 %.

Question 39 (Tasks) – Is the technical support team trained to be in charge of all platforms or is the support confined to one platform?

- 25,4 % say: The team is -like all the journalists- trained to be in charge of all platforms.
- 57,6 % say: Both are possible.
- 16,9 % say: Each individual platform has its own IT-specialists – for print and online.

Question 40 (Culture) – As to the priority between print and online: does the content determines which platform wins the audience first or is it the platform that decides on it as is customary according to "online-first"?

- 62,7 % say: The strategic distribution of contents and the question as to where these contents are most efficient are of the highest importance.
- 25,4 % say: The platform is more important. The strategic distribution of various channels, however, is being taken into consideration.
- 11,9 % say: The platform of the first publication is decisive. The contents are optimized for the platforms.
  Possible error of +/- 1,7 %.

5.2 Answers concerning the framework in organizational alignment

Based on the allocation of questions and their answers in chapter 4.2.1 the points system yields a mean average of 51.9 out of a possible 80 points for those 59 German dailies whose editors-in-chief took part in the survey. Individual results oscillate between 7 points and 75 (Abendzeitung Munich).

5.2.1 Degree of convergence, CTSP (Z), of German dailies

The mean average of 51.9 points for the participating dailies may be broken down as follows: culture, 14.5 points; tasks, 11.2 points; structure, 14.0 points; people, 12.2 points. The relation to the ideal of a fully integrated newsroom is calculated thus:

$$\text{CTSP (Z)} = \frac{\text{C (Z)} + \text{T (Z)} + \text{S (Z)} + \text{P (Z)}}{80} \times 100$$

$$\text{CTSP (59)} = \frac{14{,}5 + 11{,}2 + 14{,}0 + 12{,}2}{80} \times 100 = 65 \text{ percent.}$$

According to this computation, the 59 participating German dailies achieve a degree of print-online convergence representing 65 percent of that of the fully integrated newsroom. Transferred to the three-tiered convergence model of Kaltenbrunner et.al and Schantin the result of 65 percent convergence would suggest that within the evolutionary process the German dailies are hovering on the point of transition from the cross-medial to the integrated approach (see figure 9).

With reference to figure 6, the result may be graphically rendered like this:

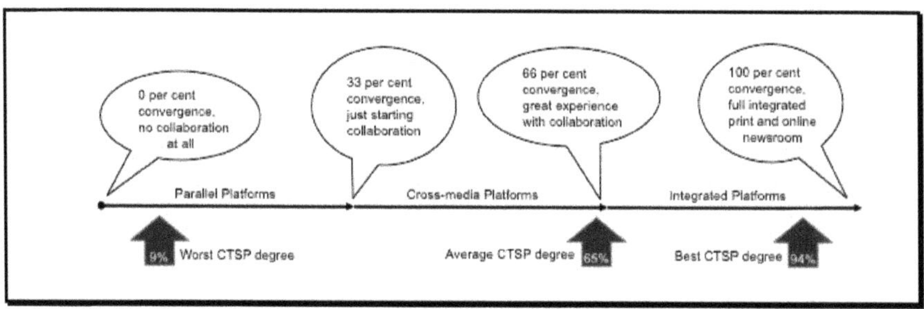

Source: Pit Gottschalk.

Figure 9: The result of CTSP-degrees according to Gottschalk

According to the information provided for the survey by the papers themselves, the Heilbronner Stimme and the Abendzeitung score highest with 94 percent. Deriving from the points system and its maximum 80 points we can establish the following ranking from No. 1 to No. 20 by CTSP-degree:

Newspapers	C	T	S	P	Σ	CTSP-degree in %
1. Abendzeitung München	19	19	18	19	**75**	**93,8**
Heilbronner Stimme	19	18	19	19	**75**	**93,8**
3. Nordwest-Zeitung	18	15	19	19	**71**	**88,8**
4. Südkurier	17	17	18	18	**70**	**87,5**
5. Schwäbische Zeitung	19	16	19	15	**69**	**86,3**
6. Ruhr-Nachrichten	16	16	17	18	**67**	**83,8**
Rhein-Zeitung	19	15	17	16	**67**	**83,8**
8. Trierischer Volksfreund	19	15	16	17	**67**	**83,8**
9. Bild-Zeitung	19	15	17	15	**66**	**82,5**
10. Hess./Niedersächsische	16	15	18	16	**65**	**81,3**
Saarbrücker Zeitung	16	16	15	18	**65**	**81,3**
Kölner Stadtanzeiger	17	15	17	16	**65**	**81,3**
13. Hamburger Abendblatt	18	14	15	17	**64**	**80,0**
14. Lausitzer Rundschau	18	16	16	13	**63**	**78,8**
15. Allgemeine Zeitung Mainz	15	16	15	15	**61**	**76,3**
16. BZ (Berlin)	17	13	16	14	**60**	**75,0**
Main-Post	15	15	14	16	**60**	**75,0**
NRZ	17	13	14	16	**60**	**75,0**
19. Nürnberger Nachrichten	16	13	16	14	**59**	**73,8**
20. Offenbach Post	14	12	18	14	**58**	**72,5**
Westfälische Nachrichten	16	12	18	12	**58**	**72,5**

Source: own survey, n = 59.

Table 2: Ranking according to CTSP-degrees

24 of the examined papers perform below the mean average degree of CTSP of 65 percent. It is crucial for an analysis of the results to look more thoroughly into the composition of the scorecard.

5.2.2 Quantifying convergence in organizational alignment

Falling back on the graphic representation introduced in chapter 4.2.3, the results can be vividly displayed on four axes (see figure 10), each of which ranges from 0 to 20 points. Connected, the four individual figures establish the visual representation of the object of study. While the black lines represent the mean average of the 59 daily papers, the grey lines represent the highest score, and the light grey line indicates the lowest.

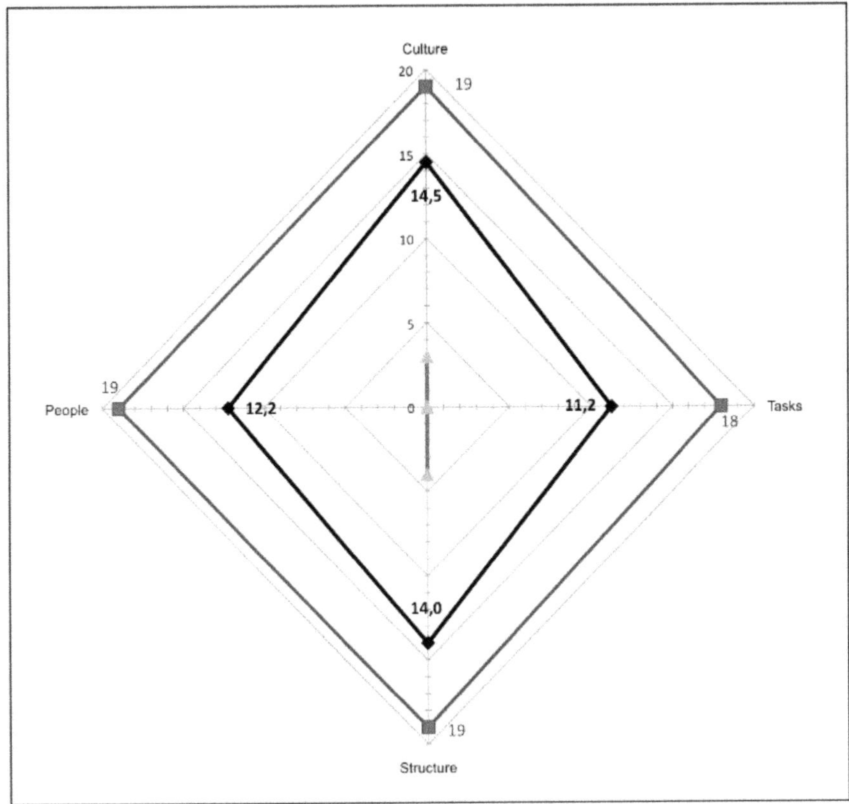

Source: own survey, n = 59.

Figure 10: Benchmarks of measurable alignment

The black lines and individual figures for culture, tasks, structure and people indicate the benchmarks for the dailies examined. Every single paper is located between the two extremes represented by the grey and light grey lines.

6. Qualitative analysis of the quantitative results

The decisive thing about an individual analysis by means of an alignment diagram is how far apart and to which direction the corresponding single values are located as compared to the components of the organizational alignment. As for the Heilbronner Stimme, each single value exceeds the average value by at least 4.5 points and by up to 6.8 points. It is obvious here that the Heilbronner Stimme does not have a deficiency with respect to the benchmark. But for reasons of optimization, the Heilbronner Stimme should have a look at those five questions which answers did not score two points: question number 7, 19, 24, 38, and 39. In these cases the Heilbronner Stimme only scored one point each. The questions in the questionnaire are designed in such a way that these minute deficiencies on the way towards a fully integrated newsroom do affect the entire organizational alignment. They can be, however, tangibly localized. The first three answers relate to journalistic practice (questions number 7 to 24) whereas the final two answers relate to "convergence plans" (questions number 34 to 40).

You can deduce from the answers in the field of journalistic practice that the staffing level at the Heilbronner Stimme is too low to optimize the division of work in an integrated newsroom. Since research, production, and distribution take place from a single source, the social network and chatting with readers have not been additionally integrated into the daily work routine yet. The answers in the field of convergence plans suggest urgency in the implementation. The employees had not been integrated into the convergence plans beforehand. They merely had been informed. Consequently, the online affinity among the technical staff varies.

This kind of inductive analytic approach of examining individual cases on the basis of gathered survey data seems to be superficial for the time being. The analysis instruments, however, offer, as in the case of the Heilbronner Stimme, initial starting points for a more profound assessment of the convergence of daily papers. The Abendzeitung München, for example, showing the same degree of CTSP (94 percent), did not score maximum points at questions number 1, 8, 18, 19, and 37 (1 point each). The answering of question number 19 (social network) is the only intersection between the Abendzeitung München and the Heilbronner Stimme. The answers of the Abendzeitung München, for one thing, relate to the newsroom where the online-first principle is not (or cannot be) generally applied. At a street sale paper the print section is highly dependent on exclusive news, which were not spread electronically before. The answers in the field of journalistic practice suggest that there is a lack of technical equipment, which is required for a full online integration. Only a part of the staff has access to the equipment, videos are partially produced by a third party rather than in-house. As to the Abendzeitung, convergence arises from editorial practical experience rather than a systematic process of learning.

The fact that even the two newspapers that can boast the best survey results in terms of a fully integrated newsroom, have a deficiency with respect to integrating the social network, can be deduced by means of the survey. In terms of online integration, the question relating to Twitter and Facebook achieved the second lowest average value among the daily newspapers.

Apparently the newspapers struggle with the online world: according to question number 22, almost 56 percent of the editors-in-chief surveyed consider the print version of a story as central whereas the online business is regarded as a tool to gain attention for the print business. This insight is in accord with the worst result in terms of online integration, the answer to question number 23. According to that, there is no necessity to independently update outdated articles on the Internet or in the archive. A journalist who is confined to print, as it seems, considers the production process completed once the article has been published. According to Jarvis, the publishing should be a new starting point for doing some research.[111]

Inductive like deductive analyses on the basis of survey results allow for localization of tangible deficiencies in terms of online integration in the print business. The analysis of the present study is conducted in two steps: firstly, the insights gained from the quantitative survey are demonstrated by reference to starting points of the survey. Secondly, the analysis is deepened by means of in-depth- interviews (all examples given relate to Axel Springer company).

6.1 Deductive analysis approach by means of the survey results

The 40 questions which were sent to editors-in-chief of German daily newspapers are set in the multiple choice format, i.e. there were three answer options for each question[112] – each answer describing a characteristic of the three given degrees of convergence.[113] Each answer was classified and – according to the degree of convergence – awarded with 0, 1 or 2 points. 0 points were given for parallel media platforms, 1 point for cross-medial working, and 2 points for online integration. The assessment of the answers presented to 59 respondents reveals that the average CTSP-degree amounts

---

[111] Cf. chapter 2.2.

[112] Cf. chapter 4.1.

[113] Cf. chapter 3.1.

to exactly 65.0 percent. Transferred to the point system of the survey, the CTSP-degree averages 1.3 points. When taking a look at the average scores achieved per question, it becomes clear that these data do not reveal a consistent picture (see figure 11). The average scores (presented on the y-axis) for each of the 40 answers (presented on the x-axis) vary considerably between 1.8 and 0.8 points.

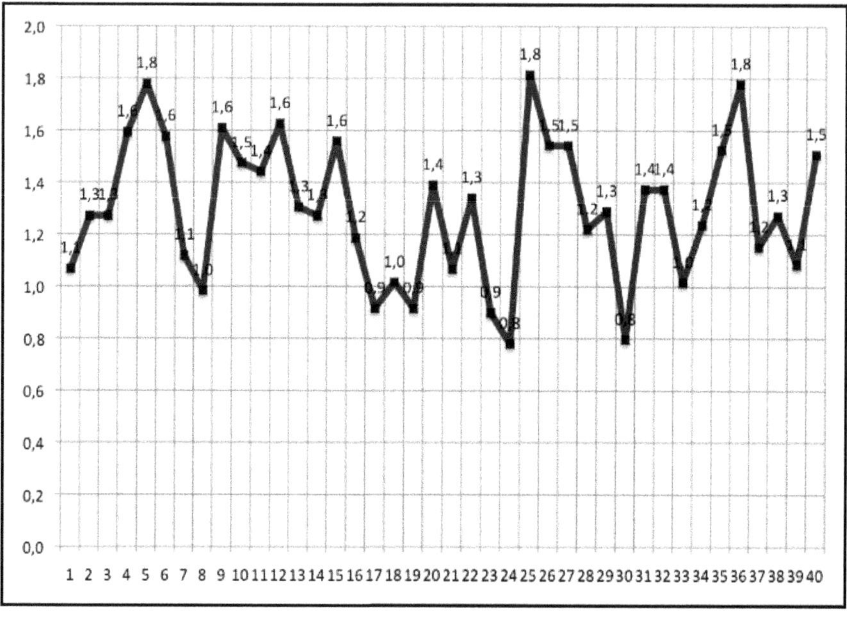

Source: own survey, n = 59.

Figure 11: Average score achieved for each survey question

The answers to the questions number 5, 25 and 36 show the highest average values whereas the answers to the questions number 24 and 30 score the lowest points on average. Unlike in the case of assessing the survey on a percentage basis (indicating how many percent of the surveyed editors-in-chief opted for each of the given answers; see chapter 5.1), the deductive analysis approach applied here allows, within the existing points system, for a fundamental assessment of the degree of convergence of all respondents with respect to each single question. Thus, it can be summarized that online integration has nearly been achieved among respondents in the following three points:

- Cooperation between media platforms is acknowledged as an integral part of the editorial processes (culture).

- Spatial proximity (defined as working in the same building) is considered a prerequisite for online integration (structure).
- Convergence is considered a fundamentally long-term process affecting the entire enterprise and each department (culture).

These findings are by no means platitudes. For years, there have been enterprises accepting or even defending spatial separation.[114] Even today print and online are considered as two independent, separate media platforms, each having its own culture.[115] It is not rare that the long-term nature of this process is accounted for by the change of culture and the resulting helplessness.[116] Not least because of this, the average CTSP-degree amounts to 65.0 percent – a value that stands for cross medial rather than integrative working. It is required to modify the working processes in order to achieve online integration. In terms of online integration, print production presupposes access to the general public via the Internet in order that editorial employees interact with their conversational partners in such a way as demanded by Jeff Jarvis. In doing so, Jarvis creates a demarcation from the existing content economy.[117] Answers that scored 0.8 or 0.9 points on average indicate that the decisive step has not been taken yet.

Average values of below 1.0 indicate, as a general rule, that the respondents failed to achieve the degree of convergence required for cross-medial working in these particular issues. With the aid of the answers to the questions number 24 and 30 as well as 17, 19, and 23, deficits in the course of online integration can be summarized as follows: According to the respondents' statements,

- print journalists fail to systematically discuss via Internet with their readers the coverage of the print version, therefore missing the opportunity to find new starting points for resuming the coverage (tasks).
- employees are not incentivized for online affinity, but rather, at best, act out of personal motivation (people).
- only one out of five employees is capable of working multimedially

---

[114] The Washington Post announced on September 17, 2009, to integrate print and online departments.

[115] Süddeutsche Zeitung in Munich employs two chief editors working separately on their platforms.

[116] After years of losses, Die Welt and its connecting local paper in Berlin (Berliner Morgenpost) had to work more effieciently by serving content on as many platforms as possible and cost-cutting at the same time.

[117] Cf. chapter 2.2

(people) and this qualification is not considered necessary nor sought after (people).

- The print sector does not feel responsible for updating online content (tasks).

The deductive derivation of these deficits in the course of online integration are in fact basic starting points for an analysis, allowing no conclusions to be drawn about individual cases when practically applying the analysis of newspapers. The comprehension of the average situation of the survey participants – this applies to the entire newspaper industry if the data are representative – serves, however, as guideline for assessing survey results of individual daily newspapers. Thus, the empirically gathered average values function as benchmark according to Haller et al.[118]

6.2 Inductive analysis using examples of three types of newspapers

Axel Springer AG is one of the media companies in Germany to have in its portfolio three types of newspapers – street sale, regional/local, and national. An inductive analysis of three types of newspapers belonging to the portfolio of one company would allow for conclusions to be drawn as to whether the degree of online integration is determined at the level of the enterprise, at the level of the publication, or at the level of the management. The inductive analysis of three daily newspapers (see chapter 6.2.1 to chapter 6.2.3) is followed by the conclusion, which critically summarizes the findings of the present study (see chapter 6.3). Contemplation of the individual newspaper (as representative of the corresponding type of newspaper) is seen in the context of assessment of convergence according to Büffel[119] and Gottschalk[120] and the application of the model for assessing convergence according to the conception of the present study. The findings of the inductive analysis will be completed, reviewed and, if necessary, relativized by on-site observation of working methods and an in-depth interview with the editor-in-chief in charge (see chapter 1.3.). This ensures the use of the conceptualized analysis instrument with the CTSP-degree for deepening the ascertained phenomena and verifying their significance. The closer look at Axel Springer's newspapers helps understand where the entire media industry, especially the newspaper companies, is going. Among the peers on

118 Cf. chapter 2.4.5.

119 Newspaper survey 2009.

120 Cf. chapter 2.4.7.

international markets, Axel Springer has proved an excellent knowledge in digitization of their business processes and meanwhile earns 21 percent of the total revenue digitally (see figure 12). This is more than the most other media companies of this size do in Europe. Just Schibsted (from Norway) is internationally ahead.

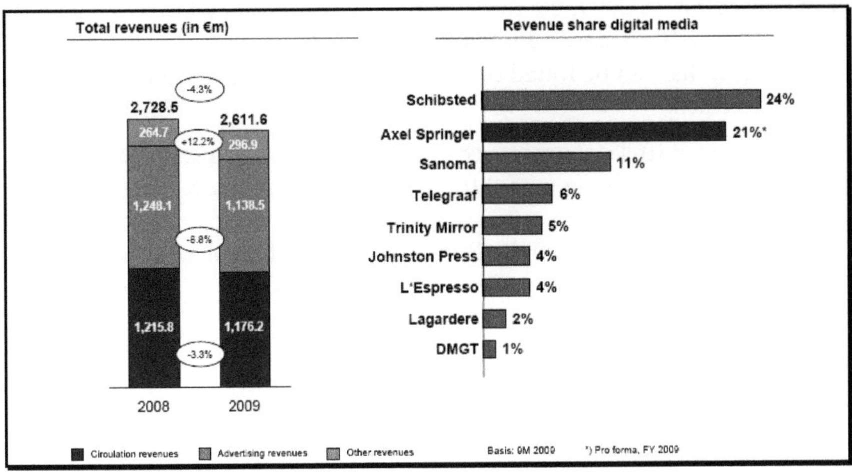

Source: Axel Springer AG.

Figure 12: Axel Springer's revenue share compared internationally

6.2.1 Street sale papers / Case study Bild

The Bild-Zeitung is a street sale paper, which was first published in 1952. According to its own account, it has become Europe's biggest selling daily newspaper. Bild is published from Monday to Saturday (except on public holidays). In 2009, 3.18 million copies[121] a day were sold on average; the reach amounted to 11.63 million readers[122]. The selling price per copy varies from region to region (between 0.50 and 0.60 euro). The number of copies distributed through subscription (subscription is confined to specific regions) amounts to 31,000.

121 According to IVW 2009.

122 According to MA II/2009.

Background of the newspaper

Kai Diekmann is editor-in-chief and publisher of the Bild-Zeitung. Also, he is one of the three managing directors at Bild digital GmbH & Co. KG, a subsidiary of Axel Springer AG. Manfred Hart, editor-in-chief at Bild digital, is editorially in charge of the online presence of the Bild-Zeitung (www.bild.de). As for disciplinary action, Manfred Hart is accountable to Kai Diekmann. In 2009, the reach of Bild digital amounted to 5.82 million unique visitors[123]. According to its own account, www.bild.de is the biggest news portal that can be found on the German-speaking Internet when it comes to reach.

According to Büffel's convergence assessment[124], out of a set of 20 Internet features the Bild-Zeitung used 8 for its Internet presence, making it 30th place among German daily newspapers. According to Gottschalk's convergence assessment[125], in 2009 the Bild-Zeitung took first place in the ranking of German daily newspapers with a web reference factor F_k (Q) of 6.08.

Interpretation of the survey results

According to the present study, the Bild-Zeitung shows a larger-than-average degree of online integration – a CTSP-degree of 82.5 percent. The maximum value of the survey was higher by 11.3 percentage points. As to the organizational alignment, the single values for all four components are above average (see figure 13). The grey lines indicate the values for Bild, the solid black lines represent the average, and the dotted lines denote the maximum value. It is conspicuous that comparatively low values of 15 points each occur in the categories tasks and people. The gap between the maximum values of the surveyed newspapers and the values of Bild amounts to three respectively four points.

---

123 According to Comscore.

124 Cf. Büffel (2009), p. 1ff.

125 Cf. Gottschalk (2009), p. 77.

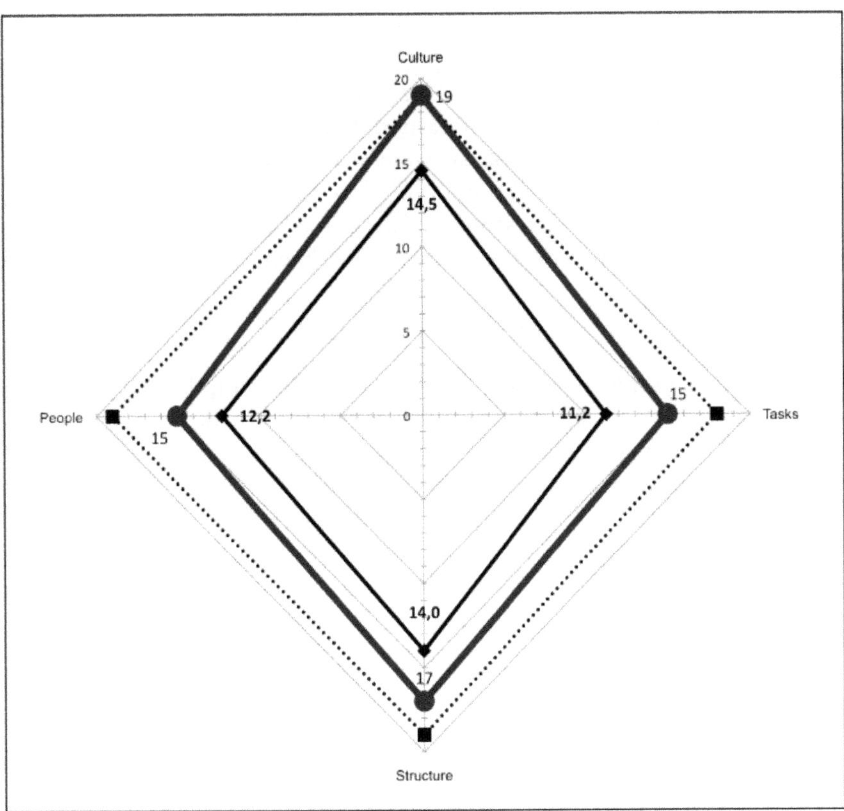

Source: own survey, n = 59.

Figure 13: Measurable alignment for Bild

A closer look at these two components in terms of the individual answers (see appendix VII) of the survey reveals that there is considerable optimization potential in the fields of newsroom and journalistic practice with respect to online integration. Thus the newsroom is the place that decides case-by-case which news are to be published online and which are to be withheld exclusively for the use of the printed media (question 1). Despite the fact that as a whole the online newsroom is integrated with the print newsroom and the information flow is high, the introduction of independent sections within the newsroom promotes an autonomous or at least dependent decision-making process (question 2). Structurally, this is the way the process is supposed to work (question 3). A separate editor-in-chief who is in charge of the online section promotes this approach. The Bild-Zeitung can afford this division of labor, which inevitably leads to a specialization in one medium (question 12). That is why experience with all media platforms is no prerequisite for working at Bild (question 16). This circumstance leads to the fact that – since not at least two thirds of the employees are capable of working on all media platforms (question 17) – updating the online archive is left to specialists (question 23) and print journalists chat online with their readers only in a given case (question 24). It fits into the picture that at the beginning multimedia journalists were increasingly sought-after (question 28) and that the technical support does not completely work convergently (question 39). The assessment of the survey results for the Bild-Zeitung within the scope of organizational alignments can be summarized as follows:

- Having achieved a CTSP-degree of 82.5 percent, the Bild-Zeitung is above average as far as convergence is concerned.
- A complete online integration in terms of newsroom and journalistic practice is not planned since a division of labor among specialists for the individual platforms is possible.
- At least a third of the employees do not work convergently.
- The culture within the Bild-Zeitung shows a high degree of online affinity
- As to tasks and employees, there is still a distinction between print and online caused by the structural preconditions.

Comparison with the observed reality in the newsroom

An on-site visit showed that a technical integration of texts without media disruptions (copy or copy and paste) is not possible from print to online or vice versa. The editorial department is prepared to produce – as one unit – two different products: a print and an online edition. It is rare that the content of the print edition is used for the online edition in identical form. The content is edited specifically for target groups or media channels. Great parts of the content are originally produced and administered for the online section. A high product range (market leadership) and the identification of the user with the brand Bild – irrespective of the kind of medium – are the goals to be achieved. In terms of space, there is no separation between print and online editors. The editors in the newsroom decide jointly or separately about the print and online appearance, both options are possible. Once the research has started the print and online editors are brought up to date about the story, they jointly follow the process of production and publication. According to Bild's account it is far more common to refer to the online edition in the print version than it is the other way round. News are published online first, they are edited for the print version.

According to the editor-in-chief, Kai Diekmann, the right strategy is to keep adjusting the work routine at Bild-Zeitung to print rather than completely to online.[126] He emphasizes that Bild records the highest profit ever with the print edition whereas the online section lacks a business model capable of achieving a similar growth. It is about making money with print for as long as possible, he says, and about achieving market leadership through online, following a strategy of organic growth. Diekmann says he cannot make a prediction as to when online will become more important than print. Due to a number of measures, it suffices for planning the future that online is a thing "that becomes second nature", Diekmann says in a conversation. According to him, the online coverage within the editorial department is a "lived routine". He presents six measures that led to the fact that online makes the Bild-Zeitung's heartbeat faster. In the present study Bild achieved a CTSP-degree of 82.5 percent.

- Bild appointed Manfred Hart as editor-in-chief at Bild digital, a man who used to work for the print version. This ensures, as Diekmann says, that the person at the top of www.bild.de is someone "who knows how Bild is functioning and who is capable of making the most of the online brand".
- The Bild-Zeitung incorporated into the royalty agreement that the editorial employees will get their bonus if online integration is promoted consciously, e.g. print journalists attending a two-week practical course in the online section, Diekmann explains.
- It is compulsory for each employee to attend a training program on the content management system of the online section, Diekmann says, "so the employees understand that there is nothing evil about it but rather (…) it embodies an important process".
- To jointly attend conferences (at least partially) has become a constant process, which promotes the mutual getting-to-know.
- Moving to Berlin and jointly using the newsroom has been a "declaration of intent right from the start" to bring together more closely print and online, Diekmann explains. It was a deliberate top-down decision, just like it was to deliberately build up pressure in order to cause a change. There are co-workers who voluntarily take an interest in new media. Then there are those you "simply have to force them to do so". The strong distinctness of a common culture resulting from the online integration is accounted for by the language usage, Diekmann argues. At Bild you do not differentiate between online or offline. Bild is considered a brand, which gains recognition at various media platforms.

---

126 Interview held on February 22, 2010.

Conclusion about the model for convergence assessment

The observations in the editorial department and the explanations of the editor-in chief are by and large in line with the core statements of the model for convergence assessment according to Gottschalk. The six measures mentioned above extensively promoted a culture according to which the online section is an integrated part of the work in the editorial department. Simultaneously, the structure intends to achieve a tight connection between print and online. The staff is sensitized for the importance of online. This does not mean, however, that at the same time online integration distracts from focusing on the highly profitable print sector. The high CTSP-degree of 82.5 percent indicates that the developmental stage of cross-medial working has been overcome. However, the stage of full integration as a consequence of a practicable strategy has not been reached yet. The comparatively low values in the categories tasks and people confirm Diekmann's intention to keep successfully running the initial core business on the one hand and to already establish the sustainability of the online section on the other hand. Bild can obviously afford the intermediate step towards a full online integration, which is to keep working with specialists for print and online.

6.2.2 Regional and local papers / Case study Hamburger Abendblatt

The Hamburger Abendblatt is a regional paper which first appeared in 1948 and which, according to its own account, became Hamburg's most widely read daily paper. The Hamburger Abendblatt appears from Monday through Saturday and, in 2009, had an average circulation of 238,568 copies[127]. This results in a coverage of 643,000 readers.[128] The cover price per copy is 1.10 euros on weekdays and 1.60 euros on Saturdays.

Background of the newspaper

The editor-in-chief of the Hamburger Abendblatt is Claus Strunz, who is simultaneously responsible for the paper's online appearance (www.abendblatt.de). In 2009 the online appearance had a coverage of 0.95 million unique visitors.[129] Mr. Strunz emphasized the intended cross – linking of the print and online sectors by means of his policy Abendblatt 3.0, published late in 2008.

---

127 According to IVW 2009.

128 According to MA 2009.

129 According to ComScore.

According to Büffel's convergence evaluation the „Hamburger Abendblatt" uses 7 out of 20 Internet features, which ranks it 43rd among German dailies. In the convergence evaluation according to Gottschalk, it came 16th in the ranking of German dailies with a web reference factor $F_k(Q)$ of 2.88.

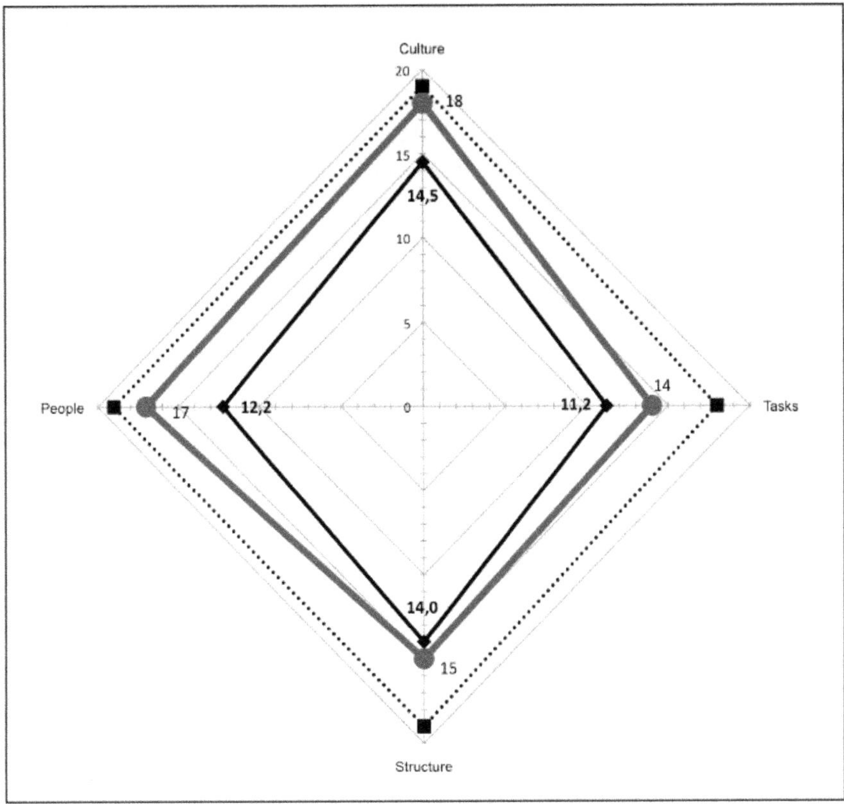

Source: own survey, n = 59.

Figure 14: Measurable alignment for Hamburger Abendblatt

Interpretation of the survey results

At a CTSP-degree of 80 percent, the study in hand established a higher than average degree of online integration for the Hamburger Abendblatt. The leading score is another 13.8 percent up. As for organizational alignment the single values of three out of the four constituents are comparatively far above average (with culture coming close to best), the exception being structure (see figure 14). The grey lines signify the data for the Hamburger Abendblatt; the black lines denote the mean average, while the dotted lines represent the maximum result. In this graph, too, the value for tasks is 2.8 points above the average, yet, at 14 points, it represents the lowest single value, 4.0 points adrift of the maximum scored. The high values for people and culture seem to argue for a marked online affinity towards integration. However, the values for structure and tasks would support assumptions that the form of organization is tendentially aligned cross-medially. The difference between informal and formal alignment would require closer scrutiny.

A more detailed appreciation of the points scored with the help of individual answers (see appendix VII) shows, with regard to the constituents structure and tasks, that in three instances the survey reveals attributes of a parallel form of organization, which is not aligned cross-medially. Research, production and release are solely tailored to the needs of a single platform and not comprehensively oriented (question 7). There is no aspiration to use moving image, no video equipment available for all staff universally (question 18), nor is the facility of independent, newsroom – based blogging considered normative (question 33). There is no incentive, such as bonus payments, to improve online affinity; everything is down to individual motivation (question 30). There is no obligation to hold joint meetings (question 4). The prevailing culture of voluntariness entails among editorial staff a propensity for not carrying out upgradings in the online sector (question 23) and promotes a merely haphazard conduct of electronic interaction with readers (question 24). Cross-linking of print and online may well be desired among the upper hierarchy – yet, among the subordinate tiers of the hierarchy convergence is not systematically implemented but, rather, it happens for reasons of practicality on the job (question 37). Evidently, there is no uniform involvement in online integration at all levels of the hierarchy, although at least two thirds of the staff at the Hamburger Abendblatt claim to be multi-medially skilled (question 17). The evaluation of the survey results may be summed up as follows:

- At a CTSP-degree of 80,0 percent, the Hamburger Abendblatt is above average regarding convergence.
- Close scrutiny reveals an inconsistent picture regarding online integration. While there exists a high degree of online affinity, there remains restriction to cross-medial structuring.
- A minimum of two thirds of the workforce is proficient at working multi-medially.

Comparison with the observed reality in the newsroom

An on-site visit revealed that an editorial department with a history of print serves both channels, print and online. Contents from the print sector are augmented, for instance by means of photo galleries, and regularly updated on the website. There is no joint content management system. There is manual transfer of texts between print and online; legally, texts may be used both in print and online. Sharing a newsroom, departmental managers coordinate the content flow between print and online. A member of staff exclusively concerned with one platform backs up each of them. Communication about a topic is run via the departmental management while the channel – specific implementation happens separately one tier down. By and large, there are more web references in print than there are references to print in the online edition.

The editor-in-chief, Claus Strunz[130], acknowledges the pressing need to restructure the workflow at a daily paper towards online integration "with a clear commitment to quality." Parallel structures between print and online "jeopardize brand identity, make for redundance and are expensive," Strunz says. The reason for the disparate impression made evident by the convergence evaluation according to Gottschalk, Strunz sees in the fact that the transformation towards working convergently is ongoing. "Not every member of staff has as yet carried over his newly – acquired online awareness into his daily routine", Strunz says. Financial perks for convergence are given exclusively to managers. Mr. Strunz added that online integration was currently tested and accounted for at executive level only. His strategy towards full online integration is to proceed with the following six measures:

- The Hamburger Abendblatt is to pool its journalistic concept irrespective of the media platforms ("one brand, one room, one team") and to control all content channels (print and online) from one multi-medially equipped newsroom.
- The responsibility for print and online is left with the department managers; press law and coordination are concentrated.
- Bonus payments are to be offered as an incentive for department managers to strive towards online integration.
- The need for cross-linking between print and online is to be aggressively communicated to the workforce to sharpen their awareness.
- The editorial staffs are obliged to phrase topic matter for online use first, and then reword it for print. Journalistic quick-wins are to illustrate the need for, and the gain by, cross-linking.
- The change management at the Hamburger Abendblatt is to be supported by education and training measures on a departmental level.

---

130 Interview held on February 25, 2010.

Conclusions about the convergence evaluation model

The observations made in the editorial office in conjunction with the deliberations of the editor-in-chief largely bear out the core statements made in the convergence evaluation model according to Gottschalk. The bundle of measures for the promotion of online integration consists of schemes with soft factors (appeals, training, quick-wins), as well as hard factors (bonus payments, concept, structure). Yet the inconsistent picture also reveals that the measures have not been evenly embraced by the staff at all the levels of the hierarchy. The high degree of online affinity (culture and people) shows that there is some sensitivity for change towards online integration. This is promoted by the spatial proximity of a shared, multi-medially equipped newsroom. The comparatively high CTSP-degree of 80,0 percent would indicate that the Hamburger Abendblatt has actually left behind the state of cross-medial working and is approaching a state of full convergence. At the same time the lower single values of structure and tasks reveal the potential for the change management to focus on structural measures that fully include all levels of the hierarchy. The status quo may be actively controlled. In terms of complete integration the status quo is an intermediary step.

6.2.3 National papers / Case study Die Welt

Die Welt is a national daily, which first appeared in 1946 and was taken over by the Axel Springer press in 1953. Die Welt appears Monday through Saturday and in 2009, in conjunction with its smaller format version Welt Kompakt, had an average circulation of 266,140 copies[131] sold and coverage of 670,000 readers[132]. It sells at 1.70 euros on weekdays and at 2.00 euros on Saturdays.

Background of the newspaper

In 2009, the then editor-in-chief Thomas Schmid, who, within the Welt group of newspapers, was simultaneously responsible for the compact format version, Welt Kompakt, the Sunday paper Welt am Sonntag, and the Internet version, Welt Online (www.welt.de). Welt Online had coverage of 3.3 million unique visitors[133] in 2009. Among German quality papers Die Welt competes with the Süddeutsche Zeitung and the Frankfurter Allgemeine Zeitung. In the convergence evaluation according to Büffel Die Welt used 12 out of 20 Internet features, which ranked it fifth among German dailies. It equally ranked fifth in the convergence evaluation according to Gottschalk with a web reference factor F_k (Q) of 4.02.

131 According to IVW 2009.

132 According to AWA 2009.

133 According to ComScore.

Interpretation of the survey results

The current study of online integration found a CTSP-degree of 66.3 percent, which puts Die Welt slightly above the mean average of 65.0 percent. This means it is 27.5 percentage points adrift of the maximum score. Regarding organizational alignment the single values for three of the four constituents, namely culture, tasks and people, are just above their respective mean averages while the value for structure is one point down on the average (see figure 15). The grey lines mark the values found for Die Welt, the black lines stand for the mean average while the dotted lines represent the maximum score. The graph makes it abundantly clear that online integration along the predefined lines is virtually non – existent. Instead, the operating principle is cross – medial such as is represented by the mean average of the papers studied (see chapter 5.2). While the culture of working convergently is, at 16 points, comparatively pronounced, there is a marked lack of integration regarding the constituent structure. This deficit in integration consequently has repercussions for tasks and people (question 7).

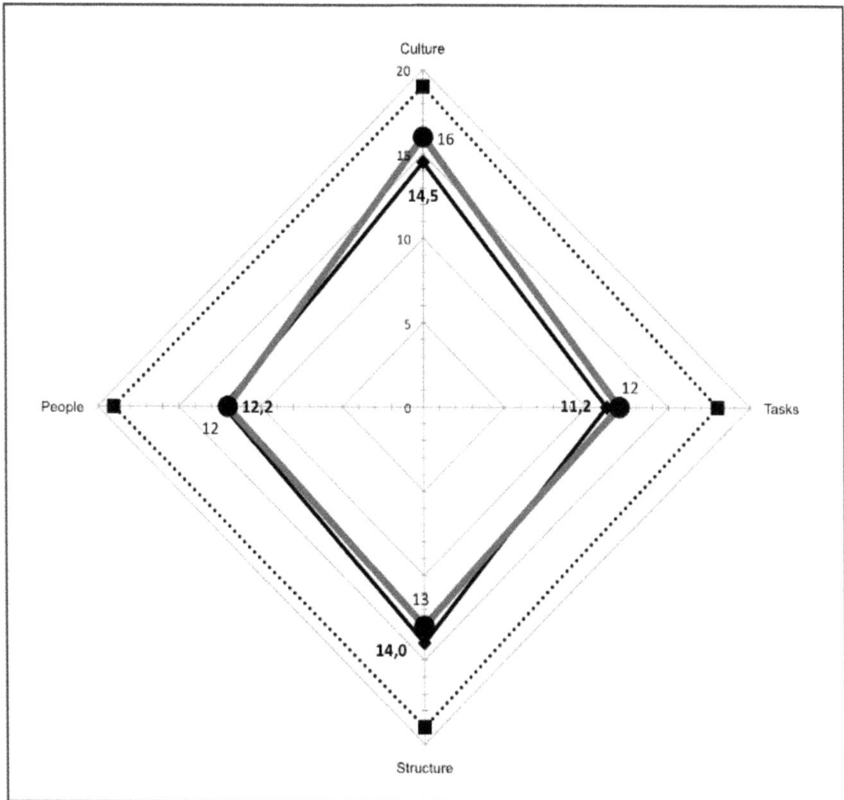

Source: own survey, n = 59.

Figure 15: Measurable alignment for Die Welt

The impression of cross-mediality in both newsroom and journalistic practice is borne out when closely examining the constituent structure by means of the individual in-depth-interviews (see appendix VII). The enquiry found that the responsibility for the co-ordination of the news flow is separated along the lines of print and online (question 3), there is no culture of mandatory participation in meetings for all editorial staff (question 4).

Accordingly, technological facilities, such as video, are not available to the entire staff (question 8). If need be, depending on the costs, videos are obtained from third – party suppliers (question 18). This structure is formative and brings about an attitude of considering information processing via social networks unnecessary and unasked – for (question 19). There are no incentives set aside for online integration which is left entirely to personal motivation (question 30), and the updating of content in the online sector is inevitably considered not part of the job description of print journalists (question 23). As a result there exist at this paper two separate spheres which are interlinked (question 2) and, in their cross-mediality, call for a high degree of co – operation and appreciation for the other platform (question 16). Yet they remain skeptical of working integratively in a shared newsroom (question 27). It follows from this that research. Production and publication are not comprehensive but centered on two separate platforms.

Regarding organizational alignment the evaluation of the survey results for the daily Die Welt can be summed up as follows:

- Die Welt is working at an average degree of convergence (CTSP-degree of 66.3 percent) and is generally leaning towards cross-medial structures.
- While there exists a marked culture for online integration, it is not implemented at an operational level. The reigning structures serve to prop up the cross – medial attitude of the staff towards their tasks.
- At least one third of the editorial staff are not working convergently.
- Online affinity persists on the level of mutual appreciation and cooperation; there is noticeable apprehension in the editorial office towards operating convergently.

Comparison with the observed reality in the newsroom

Close inspection via on-site visit revealed that in the case of Die Welt one editorial team, largely from the vantage point of print, operates both media channels, print and online. The bulk of the print content is simply put online with at best marginal alterations. Channel-specific enhancement happens to a low degree, usually via galleries or votings. Headlines are adapted for search engine purposes. There is no provision for target group-oriented enhancement of content. Licensed content material from third-party suppliers, for instance from news agencies, is used in cost-efficient ways. It follows from this set-up that the technical integration of print and online in a single content management system is not viewed as of paramount importance. Fault lines between print and online are bilaterally condoned. Since material composed for print release is manually put online according to the principle online first, staff are aware of the two-platform utilisation of their texts. No topics are suppressed, and copyright issues do not arise from this. The general acceptance that texts are inevitably published by the online sector leads to passivity and indicates that the web reference from print to online is not running satisfactorily. Conversely, the online dependence on print leads to a higher frequency of references to print.

Thomas Schmid, in 2009 editor-in-chief of the Welt group of papers, singles out two reasons why he considers online integration impeded at dailies.[134] For one thing, according to him, there is an established perception among print journalists that the online sector represents "something dodgy, a place where hackwork rules, not the environment where news are originally created." For another, he perceives a lack of media-specific formats in the online sector, which might exceed the speedy reproduction of the events of the day. Hence Mr. Schmid sees a danger in integration, namely that "under the hegemony of online the fact will be disregarded that the several media possess different rhythms and temperatures." Online was only beginning to formulate format specific offers. Thus the proper strategy is to reduce the remaining reciprocal reservations and to familiarize the cultures with one another in a prolonged process. Mr. Schmid tells of four measures designed to make cross-medial modes of operation successively lead to integration:

- Die Welt evades the pressure of implementing online integration because the Internet is perceived as supplementary, something that, according to Schmid, was „not inherent in the DNA of print." Time was needed to adapt to online.
- Part of the process of adaptation is the overcoming of reservations, such as "the mildly scornful disdain of the Internet among print journalists", adding "on both sides, hubris needs to be removed."
- The distinctions in the workflow of print and, respectively, online are kept increasingly "fluid, so that nobody may ignore the net anymore", Schmid says. While it was possible to confine one's work to the print sector, there had to emerge awareness online existed.

134 Interview held on February 24, 2010.

- Die Welt is not considering a system which rewards convergent operations, yet there was no way of getting past "establishing a regime which will sanction whosoever does not think in online categories", Schmid explains. These sanctions are understood to take the shape of an internal kind of shaming.

Conclusions about the convergence evaluation model

In its measures to promote convergence Die Welt favors the time factor and backs soft factors in its bid to bring about a change of attitude. Since the decision, in 2005, under the predecessors of Mr. Schmid, to produce various publications utilizing the synergetic effects of a shared newsroom, comparable structural measures have been wanting. The assessment of the status quo reveals a need for action if the aim is to promote integration. At a CTSP-degree of 66.3 percent Die Welt operates with a leaning towards cross-mediality. Unlike at Bild, integration is not promoted via a system of incentives or via targets as to the job descriptions that are imposed top-down and then filled with life. The editor-in-chief acts as a mediator between two separate worlds striving to unite their several cultures under a single brand of quality journalism. The rapprochement has apparently advanced to a point where online affinity is conceived as a shared cultural asset scoring comparatively well in the convergence model. However, structural measures would have to include tasks and people and would need to be shored up by hard factors such as a remunerative system and operational merging.

6.3 Brief summary of the assessment of convergence

For each of the three daily newspapers of Axel Springer AG the two weakest components of the organizational alignment model are depicted in a matrix. It becomes obvious that the three daily newspapers – despite the fact that the management is the same (they are all part of Axel Springer AG) – not only show different CTSP-degrees but also different starting points in terms of organization in order to complete the online integration (table 3).

Axel Springer newspapers	C	T	S	P
Bild-Zeitung (82,5 %)		√		√
Hamburger Abendblatt (80,0 %)		√	√	
Die Welt (66,3 %)			√	√

Source: own survey.

Table 3: Comparison in terms of CTSP-weaknesses at Axel Springer

Thus, the reason is to be found in the management of the publication (chief editorship) and in the nature of the type of newspaper. The fact that all three publications are characterized by a culture of online affinity (this is not a weak point of a publication) can be seen from the matrix, just as the conclusion that the implementation has not completely been carried out in terms of structure (Hamburger Abendblatt and Die Welt), in terms of personnel (Bild and Die Welt), and in terms of operation (Bild and Hamburger Abendblatt). The data and starting points that resulted from the analysis can be used to improve online integration. These findings are helpful for preparing for questions relating to the future, which the newspaper publishing companies will have to face in the digital age. The model for assessing convergence, which was conceptualized during the course of the present study, fulfills the requirements of the research objective.

7. Conclusion

The research objective as stated in chapter 1.2. can be divided into three parts whose fulfillment will be shown and assessed individually below.

The research objective is to develop a concept for assessing the degree of convergence between print and online in editorial offices.

Fulfilled. The present study extended the survey framework of the existing model for assessing convergence according to Kaltenbrunner et al. by practice-oriented questions. Also, an empirical evaluation method for generating comparable data sets was incorporated into the existing multiple-choice format. Having considered all evaluation methods, which are available in the literature, it becomes obvious that the conceptual approach for graphically depicting convergence between print and online on an empirical basis is new and unique.

The degree of online integration for newspaper production in Germany is to be evaluated on a quantitative basis …

Fulfilled. With the aid of the model for assessing convergence, the degree of online integration was deduced from the edited data sets and expressed in percentage points (CTSP-degree). Maximum values and average values establish benchmarks, which allow comparability towards online integration – at least at the level of survey respondents.

… in order to analyze the existing forms of organization of German daily newspapers according to the model of organizational alignment (culture, tasks, people, structure) and to develop a fundamental analysis instrument.

Fulfilled. On the basis of the survey results and by means of the CTSP-degree, the developed model for assessing convergence simulates in a sophisticated manner the orientation within the form of organization. The inductive analysis by means of the model for assessing convergence produces practice-oriented starting points for deepening the investigation of online integration and for improving the convergence between print and online in the daily newspaper business.

Based on the self-disclosures of the editors-in-chiefs, the present study deals with the convergence of German daily newspapers. The findings can be summarized as follows:

- According to the given definition of convergence (CTSP-degree), the online-integrative work of the 59 German daily newspapers that participated in the survey amounts to 65 percent on average.
- The two daily newspapers with the highest degree of online integration show a degree of convergence of 93.8 percent (Heilbronner Stimme and Abendzeitung München), whereas the newspaper with the lowest degree of online integration shows a degree of convergence of 8.8 percent.
- Based on the survey results, the deductive analysis approach allows for defining maximum values and benchmarks for the survey respondents (for the entire newspaper industry if the data are representative) by means of which individual results can be compared.
- According to the organizational alignment model online affinity of the 59 survey participants is strongest at culture (14.5 out of 20 points) and structure (14.0 out of 20 points), weakest at people (12.2 out of 20 points) and tasks (11.2 out of 20 points).
- The deductively obtained analysis results are to be deepened by means of inductive analysis. Sharpening the profile of online affinity by means of individual survey answers achieves this.

7.1 Strong and weak points of the model for assessing convergence

Two parameters are decisive for the significance of the model for assessing convergence: firstly, the number of editors-in-chief participating in the survey in order to generate at best representative benchmarks. Secondly, the assignment of the questions to the four components of the organizational alignment in order that conclusions as to the editorial reality can be drawn from the empirical survey. With 59 daily newspapers having participated in the survey, the present study accounts for 16.8 percent of all German daily newspapers in terms of degree of online integration. The question as to whether the average CTSP-degree of 65.0 percent is actually representative can only be answered by means of statistical investigations. The present study explicitly differentiated between newspapers that participated in the survey and the entire German newspaper industry in order to avoid premature conclusions. It is not unlikely, however, that the ascertained results are generally valid. The assignment of the questions to the four components of the organizational alignment was made on the basis of the author's many years' practical experience in the newspaper business and understanding of forms of organizations as taught by Doug Guthrie, Academic Director of the Berlin School of Creative Leadership.[135] Random checks among the editors-in-chief who participated in the survey confirm the logic of the assignment. As for future investigations, transparency of the assignment of the questions is urgently needed in order to, if necessary, carry out adaptations on the basis of the feedback received. Furthermore, it should be noted that questions must be adapted to possible developments in technology. Regarding online integration, it is well possible that an integration of mobile phone technology needs to be considered. Due to its display and the usage of a mobile phone, this technology requires another form of editing the news content. Furthermore, it is important to be prepared for dealing with developments, namely those that consider the clientele as a composition of individual target groups, which individually need to be approached with content. This is contrary to the approach taken in the present study, which regards the clientele as a unit (readership or community). Beyond online integration, this kind of development would require forms of organization, which are capable of implementing a target group-related news distribution and extending production methods. It is all the more important to consider the issue of online integration, as thematized in the present study, an important intermediate goal that is to be achieved. The strong points of the model for assessing convergence at the back end (just as is the case for front end) can be summarized as follows:

- Comparability of own online affinity in the daily newspaper to the sector by means of web references is comprehensible and testable.
- It offers change management new starting points for measuring and accelerating in the development of convergence with the Internet.
- Another possibility to balance qualitative and quantitative features and assessments.

As to the model for assessing convergence, the weak points were identified:

- The assessment of convergence solely focuses on the frank answers of the daily newspapers' editors-in-chief.
- Online affinity in daily newspapers is measured without direct analysis of the content.

---

135 Cf. Guthrie (2009), http://www.berlin-school.com/nc/ideas/video/catid/graduation_films/category/graduation_films/video/doug_guthrie_graduation_speech/ (as of March 22, 2010).

- Questions of detail related to lower levels in hierarchy are being ignored.

By contrast, the prospects for the model for assessing convergence are the following:

- Dealing with symbiosis of print and online in an offensive way.
- Visible and provable quick wins for change management in the course of digitization of daily newspapers.
- Starting points or approaches for further studies on the complementary relation between print and online as well as transformational processes.

As to the model for assessing convergence, two points in particular can be considered as risks:

- The results produced by the assessment models are incorrect when implementing superficially and at short notice integration measures within editorial departments.
- As to the structure of the survey, the balance between qualitative and quantitative features is criticizable.

7.2 Perspective and starting points for further studies

The obtained average values for the CTSP-degree and the components of the organizational alignment are to be consolidated quantitatively by increasing the number of survey participants until statistical significance is reached; qualitatively by controlling, updating or adjusting the composition of the survey questions. A repeat of the present study at a later point of time could test the existing procedure for assessing convergence in order to either make corrections to the procedure or to discover that online affinity at daily newspapers indeed has increased. Following the model of inductive analysis, as has been done in the case of the three Axel Springer newspapers, more daily newspapers could be the basis for further investigations.

If in the transformation of newspapers phenomena of the same origin are to be identified, the reasons should be clustered and categorized. In this way, by stringing together individual cases, general recommendations for action can be made, which go beyond those recommendations currently available in specialist literature. Moreover, comparisons with foreign markets are helpful to examine whether there are differences in terms of start, duration and intensity of the transformational process in the newspaper industry. A starting point for further investigations could be to integrate into the investigation on online integration of newspaper publishing companies the sectors typical to the industry: distribution and advertising sales.

8. Bibliography

Anding, M./ Hess, T. (2003): Was ist Content? Zur Definition und Systematisierung von Medieninhalten. In: Arbeitspapiere des Instituts für Wirtschaftsinformatik und Neue Medien, Nummer 5/03, LMU (Hrsg.), Munich.

Büffel, St./ Spang, S. (2008): Zeitungen Online 2008. In: media-ocean, http://bit.ly/9ANXZI [March 8, 2010], Cologne.

Büffel, St. (2008): Eckdaten zur Studie Zeitungen Online 2008. In: Medien- und Verlagsberatung Steffen Büffel, Media- Ocean (Hrsg.), Cologne.

Büffel, St. (2009): Zeitungen Online 2009. In: Forschung, http://www.media-ocean.de/forschung/ [March 8, 2010], Cologne.

Campbell, C. (2008): Der Weg des Daily Telegraph zur Konvergenz. In: Special Report of Ifra GmbH & Co. KG (Hrsg.), Darmstadt.

Dailey, L./ Demo, L./ Spillman, M. (2003): The Convergence Continuum: A Model for Studying Collaboration between Media Newsrooms. In: Submitted to the Newspaper Division of the Association for Education in Journalism and Mass Communication, Kansas City, Missouri (USA).

Friedrichsen, M. (2007): Presse im Wandel. In: Vortrag 5. Oktober 2007, Cologne.

Garcia, M. (2008): The Path of the Story: From Mobile to Online to Print. In: Garciamedia, http://bit.ly/bEr8r9 [March 8, 2010], Tampa, USA.

Gottschalk, P. (2007): Der perfekte Nachwuchsjournalist. In: Traumberuf Sportjournalist, Michael Schaffrath (Hrsg.), LIT Verlag, Berlin.

Gottschalk, P. (2009): Der kreative Link von Print zu Online – Erhebung über die Zahl der Möglichkeiten für Webverweise in deutschen Tageszeitungen. Steinbeis University, Berlin/Stuttgart.

Guthrie, D. (2009): Graduation speech at Berlin School of Creative Leadership. In: website of Berlin School of Creative Leadership, http://www.berlin-school.com/nc/ideas/video/catid/graduation_films/category/graduation_films/ video/doug_guthrie_graduation_speech/ [March 22, 2010], Berlin.

Haller, M. (2004): Anamnese – Diagnose – Therapie: Mit Benchmarking aus der Krise. In: Separatum zum Geschäftsbericht der Deutschen Druck- und Verlagsgesellschaft mbH (DDVG), Hamburg.

Jarvis, J. (2009): Was würde Google tun? Wilhelm Heyne Verlag, Munich.

Johnson, J. (2008): The Use of the Internet by America's Largest Newspapers. In: The Bivings Report, http://bit.ly/by83Bv [March 8, 2010], Washington, DC, USA.

Kahlmann, A. (2009): Stimmt es, dass Print zerrinnt? Eine CEO-Studie zu den Verlagsstrukturen der Zukunft, Unternehmensberatung Schickler (Hrsg.), Hamburg.

Kaltenbrunner, A./ Meier, K./ Garcia Avilés, J./ Kraus, D./ Carvajal, M. (2009): Newsroom-Konvergenz in Tageszeitungen im internationalen Vergleich, In: Die österreichische Medienlandschaft im Umbruch, p. 261–294, Birgit Stark und Melanie Magin (Hrsg.), Vienna.

Kansky, H. (2009): Kreativ durch die Krise – Zur Entwicklung der digitalen Geschäftsfelder. In: Alles. Jederzeit. Überall. Zeitung online und mobil – zum Stand der Dinge, p. 5–16, BDZV / Anja Pasquay (Hrsg.), Berlin.

Keller, D. (2009): Schwierige Zeiten – Zur wirtschaftlichen Lage der deutschen Zeitungen. In: Zeitungen 2009, p. 29–106, BDZV (Hrsg.), Berlin.

Köcher, R. (2008): Die Entwicklung von Print in der digital geprägten Medienwelt. In: VDZ-Jahrbuch ´08, p. 18–22, VDZ (Hrsg.), Berlin.

Kramer, S. (2009): Updated: Washington Post Online, Print Operations Will Merge Jan. 1, 2010. In: PaidContent.Org, http://bit.ly/3gzIYN [March 8, 2010], New York.

Krell, S. (2008): Zukunft der Zeitung. Katholische Universität, Eichstaedt.

Lafrenz, R./ Schlankardt, F./ Moring, A. (2009): Konzept zur Restrukturierung der Redaktionen – Betriebsversammlung Westdeutsche Allgemeine Zeitung, http://files1.derwesten.de/pdf/Praesentation_WAZ_ Betriebsversammlung_2009-03-04.pdf [March 8, 2010].

Mahrdt, N. (2008): Audience Flow. In: Media Economics, http://bit.ly/4tieOe [March 8, 2010], Cologne.

Meyer, K. (2005): Crossmediale Kooperation von Print- und Online-Redaktionen bei Tageszeitungen in Deutschland. Herbert Utz Verlag, Munich.

Mogg, A./ Franke, B./ Seibert, C./ Veer, C. (2008): There's life in the old dog yet – Print media in the digital age. In: Strategy Consulting Roland Berger (Hrsg.), Munich.

Nadler D./ Tushman, M. (1997): Competing by Design: The Power of Organizational Architectures. Oxford University Press, New York.

Pirker, H./ Bauer, D./ Buchsteiner, I./ Granigg, W. (2009): Die drei Leben einer Tageszeitung. Transformation des klassischen Geschäftsmodells. In: Report Nummer 9, research projects called "Where News?" of Ifra GmbH & Co. KG (Hrsg.), Darmstadt.

Project for Excellence in Journalism (2008): The Changing Newsroom: What is Being Gained and What is Being Lost in America's Daily Newspapers. http://www.journalism.org/node/11961 [December 18, 2010], Washington, DC, USA.

Project for Excellence in Journalism (2009): State of the News Media Report. http://www.stateofthemedia.org/2009/index.htm [December 18, 2010], Washington, DC, USA.

Riepl, W. (1913): Das Nachrichtenwesen des Altertums mit besonderer Rücksicht auf die Römer. Teubner, Leipzig.

Rogers, M. (2006): Technology Is Now an Important Part of Media. Interview with Patrick Phillips. In: I Want Media, http://www.iwantmedia.com/people/ people62.html [March 8, 2010], New York.

Rosen, J. (2009): "Es ist alles keine Katastrophe". In: Wozu noch Zeitungen? Wie das Internet die Presse revolutioniert, p. 170–181, Verlag Vandenhoeck & Ruprecht, Goettingen.

Roth, J. (2005): Internetstrategien von Lokal- und Regionalzeitungen, University Bremen.

Schantin, D./ Juul, T./ Meier, K. (2007): Crossmediale Redaktionen in Deutschland. In: Special Report der Ifra GmbH & Co. KG (Hrsg.), Darmstadt.

Schantin, D. (2009): Newsrooms 1-2-3. In: Newsplex Europe – review and outlook, p. 8f., WAN/Ifra (Hrsg.), Darmstadt.

Schantin-Williams, S. (2007): Reorganization in der Redaktion: Change-Management-Grundlagen. In: Special Report der Ifra GmbH & Co. KG (Hrsg.), Darmstadt.

Schulze, V. (2004): 50 Jahre Bundesverband Deutscher Zeitungsverleger. In: Festschrift 50 Jahre BDZV, p. 20–41, Berlin.

Schmalz G. (2009), Die Online-Generation ist politisch. In: FR-online.de (Frankfurter Rundschau), Interview mit Peter Hanack, http://bit.ly/4bch5F [November 02, 2009], Frankfurt/M.

Schneider, V. (2009): Alle Nachrichten über einen Tisch. In: Message, 01/2009, p. 80–83, Michael Haller (Hrsg.), Leipzig.

Vidal-Folch, X. (2009): Introduction. In: Trends in Newsrooms 2009, p. IV, WAN (Hrsg.), Paris.

Weichert, St./ Kramp, L./ Jakobs, H.-J. (2009): Wozu noch Zeitungen? Wie das Internet die Presse revolutioniert. Vandenhoeck & Ruprecht, Goettingen.

Wiele, A. (2009): "Man muss Schmerzen ausmerzen" – Axel-Springer-Vorstand Andreas Wiele über die Stärke der Gattung Print. Interview with Julia Paperlein und Roland Pimpl. In: Horizont, 5/2009, p. 24ff., Deutscher Fachverlag, Frankfurt/Main.

Zogby, J. (2008): Newsroom culture has changed: multimedia, multiskilled will bet he norm. In: Trends in Newsrooms 2008, p. 1–11, WAN (Hrsg.), Paris.

Internet sources

http://events.apple.com.edgesuite.net/1001q3f8hhr/event/index.html [as of March 8, 2010]

http://bit.ly/cYRmDM [as of March 8, 2010]

http://www.bdzv.de/schaubilder+M51fb47b30df.html [as of March 8, 2010]

http://w4.stern.nyu.edu/faculty/facultyindex.cgi?id=348 [as of March 8, 2010]

http://www.nacdny.org/PDF/bio_nadler.pdf [as of March 8, 2010]

http://bit.ly/9P6MPU [as of March 8, 2010]

http://www.medienhaus-wien.at/cgi-bin/page.pl?id=13 [as March 8, 2010]

http://www.buzzmachine.com/about-me/ [as of March 8, 2010]

http://www.buzzmachine.com

http://garciamedia.com/about/bio/dr_mario_r_garcia [as of March 8, 2010]

http://bit.ly/bEr8r9 [as of March 8, 2010]

http://bit.ly/3gzIYN [as of March 8, 2010]

http://www.iwantmedia.com/people/people62.html [as of March 8, 2010]

http://journalism.nyu.edu/faculty/rosen.html [as of March 8, 2019)

http://de.wikipedia.org/wiki/Stephan_Weichert [as of March 8, 2010]

http://www.ifd-allensbach.de/ [as of March 8, 2010]

http://files1.derwesten.de/pdf/Praesentation_WAZ_Betriebsversammlung_2009-03-04.pdf [as of March 8, 2010]

https://www.xing.com/profile/Mike_Friedrichsen [as of March 8, 2010]

http://www.yeseconomy.net/?page_id=18 [as of March 8, 2010]

http://bit.ly/4bch5F [as of March 8, 2010]

https://www.xing.com/profile/Sonja_Krell [as of March 8, 2010]

http://journalism.unr.edu/faculty-staff//app-faculty/6/larry-dailey/ [as of March 8, 2010]

http://bit.ly/by83Bv [as of March 8, 2010]

http://www.media-ocean.de/forschung/ [as of March 8, 2010]

http://bit.ly/9ANXZI [as of March 8, 2010]

http://www.media-ocean.de/forschung/ [as of March 8, 2010]

http://www.unileipzig.de/journalistik/haller.htm [as of March 8, 2010]

http://www.kindermedienagentur.com/roth.htm [as of March 8, 2010]

http://bit.ly/4tieOe [as of March 8, 2010]

http://www.berlin-school.com/nc/ideas/video/catid/graduation_films/category/graduation_films/video/doug_guthrie_graduation_speech/ [as of March 22, 2010]

Abbreviations

AWA	Allensbacher Markt- und Werbeträger-Analyse (market research)
BDZV	Bundesverband Deutscher Zeitungsverleger e.V.
CEO	Chief Executiv Officer
CMS	Content Management System
CTSP	Degree of culture, tasks, structure, people
Cf.	Confer
DLD	Digital, Life, Design conference
e.g.	exempli gratia (for example)
et al.	et alii (and others)
etc.	et cetera (and so on)
f.	and the following page
ff.	and the following pages
Hrsg.	Publisher
i.e.	id est (that means)
n	Numbers of participants applied
OECD	Organization for Economic cooperation and Development
p.	Page
resp.	respective
TV	Television
URL	Uniform Resource Locator
VDZ	Verband Deutscher Zeitschriftenverleger e.V.
WAN	World Association of Newspapers and News Publishers
WAZ	Westdeutsche Allgemeine Zeitung

www.ingramcontent.com/pod-product-compliance
Ingram Content Group UK Ltd.
Pitfield, Milton Keynes, MK11 3LW, UK
UKHW020200200726
13856UKWH00003B/1096

9 781446 687383